T0243896

a **FUTURE** *for* *the* **FISHERY**

Crisis and Renewal in Canada's Neglected Fishing Industry

Rick Williams

Foreword by Donald Savoie

NIMBUS
PUBLISHING
—— NIMBUS.CA ——

Copyright © 2019, Rick Williams

All rights reserved. No part of this book may be reproduced, stored in a retrieval system or transmitted in any form or by any means without the prior written permission from the publisher, or, in the case of photocopying or other reprographic copying, permission from Access Copyright, 1 Yonge Street, Suite 1900, Toronto, Ontario M5E 1E5.

Nimbus Publishing Limited
3660 Strawberry Hill Street, Halifax, NS, B3K 5A9
(902) 455-4286 nimbus.ca

Printed and bound in Canada

NB1501

Design: Jenn Embree
Editor: Paula Sarson
Editor for the press: Angela Mombourquette
Proofreader: Elizabeth Eve

Library and Archives Canada Cataloguing in Publication

Title: A future for the fishery : crisis and renewal in Canada's neglected fishing industry / Rick Williams ; foreword by Donald Savoie.
Names: Williams, Rick, 1945- author.
Description: Includes bibliographical references and index.
Identifiers: Canadiana 20190169362 | ISBN 9781771088053 (softcover)
Subjects: LCSH: Fisheries—Canada. | LCSH: Fisheries—Economic aspects—Canada.
Classification: LCC SH223 .W55 2019 | DDC 338.7/63920971—dc23

Nimbus Publishing acknowledges the financial support for its publishing activities from the Government of Canada, the Canada Council for the Arts, and from the Province of Nova Scotia. We are pleased to work in partnership with the Province of Nova Scotia to develop and promote our creative industries for the benefit of all Nova Scotians.

To Lauren, Jonathan, and Diane—in gratitude for your support and your tolerance for my many absences.

CONTENTS

FOREWORD

The fishery and Atlantic Canada are tied at the hip. The fishery first attracted Europeans to our shores in search of a better life. It then gave life to some one thousand communities in Atlantic Canada and continues to be the economic backbone in many of those communities. The fishing industry also constitutes an important component of Atlantic Canada's exports, and many in the region now look to the agri-food sector, of which the fishery is an important component, as one of the region's key growth sectors.

As is well known, however, the fishery is looking at a number of daunting challenges. These include global warming, depletion of several species, rivalries over access to the fish, conflicts over resource allocation, transportation costs, and international competition. Rick Williams, in his well-researched and well-written study, points to another important challenge, one that is all too often overlooked. This is surprising, given that it is arguably the sector's most important challenge, one that goes to the heart of the economic future of many rural communities.

Williams sums up the challenge nicely: "enough fish, not enough fishermen." In twenty years or so, we have flipped the challenge from "too many fishermen, not enough fish" to "too many fish, not enough fishermen." At the risk of stating the obvious, communities depend on individuals, particularly the most industrious ones, to grow and prosper. Nowhere is this more evident than in rural communities, and no sector is as important to the rural communities dotting the shoreline in the four Atlantic provinces as the fishery sector.

Rural Canada can only prosper if we make it attractive for younger generations to stay. This is where the fishery sector, indeed the whole food industry, comes in. Rick Williams pulls no punches in this important study that looks at several facets of the industry but focuses on human resources. He documents the demographic challenges confronting the fishing industry and fishing communities. However, unlike so many studies of this genre, he is not content with outlining the challenges; he offers a series of solutions to attract workers to the fishery.

Rick Williams has produced an excellent and timely study to address the most important challenge facing the fishing industry. This book should be of strong interest to policy-makers, students of public policy, government officials in both Ottawa and provincial capitals, community leaders in Atlantic Canada, those employed in the fishery, and those who are looking to the fishery for either economic or employment opportunities.

Donald J. Savoie
Canada Research Chair in
Public Administration and Governance
Université de Moncton

PREFACE

I have three goals for this book.

The first is that I have recently completed four years of intensive research on issues and trends in the Canadian fishing industry and I want to make the findings available to and more accessible for a wider audience. The project report is a dry recitation of evidence, heavily laden with tables and charts, and not something that many would enjoy slogging through. This book is an attempt to draw out a clearer narrative from the mass of statistical data and qualitative findings so that people who work in the sector will more readily find themselves in it, and so that leaders and interested observers in industry, government, and rural communities may better understand and possibly act on the challenges and opportunities taking shape throughout the industry.

A second motivation is to share some of my own reflections after more than four decades of working in and around the Canadian fishing industry. The evidence reviewed in this book suggests that the fishing industry is approaching a crisis point where long-term demographic and labour market trends may tip over into rapid and steep decline with devastating impacts on coastal communities and regional economies. The situation calls for new strategies and creative policy and program interventions. Having been a close observer and sometimes active participant in fisheries policy issues since the mid-1970s, I have ideas to share on how we might arrive at a more socially, economically, and ecologically sustainable future for the fishery.

My third motivation is to challenge certain public attitudes about the fishery and what I see as a pattern of complacency bordering on benign neglect by federal and provincial governments. There is not, I observe, a high level of awareness among the wider Canadian public of the contributions the industry makes in generating jobs, incomes, and export earnings and in supplying healthy food products to consumers in local, national, and global markets. Urban folk take for granted their enjoyment of coquilles St. Jacques in white-table restaurants, or Filet-O-Fish burgers at McDonald's, without thinking much about the role of the fishery in sustaining many hundreds of unique and culturally vibrant coastal and First Nations communities. Fishing families populate coastal regions that might otherwise be unoccupied and neglected, and the harvesters have become primary stewards of marine ecosystems. Without their data generation and observational knowledge gained over decades of work on the water it would be impossible for fisheries managers and scientists to track changes in fish stocks and habitats and the marine environment.

But it is rare to hear clear and sincere recognition of these contributions, and rarer still to see serious commitments to sustaining them. I have observed this reality over many years without finding clear explanations for it. Part of the blame must fall on industry itself, which in some regions is poorly organized and internally divided with a poor record of standing up for itself. In two provinces in particular, Nova Scotia and British Columbia, there are still no strong umbrella organizations to bring harvesters together and give them a voice.

In my home province of Nova Scotia, the fishery employs many more people and generates six times more export earnings than the farming sector, but provincial program spending on fisheries is well under half the $50 million allocated to agriculture. Whenever I get the chance, I ask politicians and senior bureaucrats why the fishery gets such short shrift in the province. The most frequent answer has been that farmers have always been well organized and politically influential through their provincial Federation of Agriculture while the fishery is largely silent and invisible at the political and policy level. Nova Scotia is perhaps the most extreme example, but similar patterns are evident in other fishing provinces.

Another important barrier to fisheries development has been divided jurisdiction. At Confederation, the British North America Act left provinces with responsibility for everything happening on land, including fish processing, education and training, and industry organization, while the federal government had authority over international trade, regulation of fishing fleets, and protection of fish resources and the marine environment. For many years, the federal Department of Fisheries and Oceans (DFO) did make significant investments in fisheries research and development and trade expansion, but that ended with the government-wide program review in 1996 that narrowed the department's mandate to protecting and conserving fish stocks. Since then, there has been no lead agency to coordinate planning and development efforts across the whole industry in Canada and little willingness to invest significant resources in such efforts. This lack of policy integration and leadership is, I believe, particularly problematic today when the industry is experiencing dramatic economic expansion but also faces a looming labour supply crisis.

While I was a deputy minister in the Government of Nova Scotia in 2012, I attended a meeting on a strategy to promote the oceans sector as an economic growth driver for the province. Senior policy staff listed opportunities in shipbuilding, electronics, defence technologies, and aquaculture, all of which together were generating about $300 million in exports at the time. The commercial fishery was not on the list. When I asked why, reminding them that the industry was then the leading export sector with $1.5 billion in earnings for the province, there was silence around the table. Someone then suggested that the fishery was a "mature industry" and not a target for innovation;

another said that fisheries development was a federal responsibility. This example—one of dozens of similar experiences I could share—illustrates the marginalized position of fish harvesting as an economic sector: it receives token attention in most provincial governments, has been a low priority at the federal level, and its current contributions and growth potential get lost in between.

There are indications of a recent change in attitudes in Nova Scotia and beyond. The expansion of specialized facilities at the Halifax and Moncton airports has contributed significantly to the growth of international lobster exports, the Atlantic Fisheries Fund announced in 2017 is providing some $400 million in funding for research and innovation projects, and the British Columbia Salmon Restoration and Innovation Fund (2018) will do the same in that province.[1] I would still question whether the harvesting sector is receiving the attention and support it merits given its current and potential contributions to economic renewal in disadvantaged regions.

Yet another important factor shaping fisheries policy in Canada is the politically disadvantaged position of the Atlantic provinces within the Canadian federation. Regional development expert Donald Savoie has convincingly challenged the progressive centralization of the federal government bureaucracy and the many ways in which Canadian politics and policy-making are dominated by the interests of the larger provinces. In his 2017 book, *Looking for Bootstraps: Economic Development in the Maritimes*, Savoie succinctly frames this issue: "For well over a century, the federal government has failed to accommodate regional economic circumstances in shaping national policies simply because Canada's political institutions were not designed to accommodate regional circumstances. That the nation's capital is located in Ottawa and more and more federal government officials are located in the NCR [National Capital Region] in recent years have not helped matters."[2]

These two sentences accurately describe governance for the fishing industry in Canada. The most important decisions impacting fishing activities and business viability for fish harvesters on both the

Atlantic and Pacific coasts are made on the upper floors of a greenish office tower on Kent Street in Ottawa, DFO's national headquarters. I have met and worked with officials there who do indeed work hard to understand and act on industry needs and aspirations, but their capacities to respond are tightly constrained by the directions emanating from the Treasury Board, the Privy Council Office, or the Prime Minister's Office. What goes on in the fishery is just not that important in the Ottawa world surrounding the green building.

Consistent with Savoie's observations, few of the major advances in the Canadian fishery that I have observed since the 1970s have been initiated and carried forward by Ottawa bureaucrats and policy experts with deep commitments to developing the fisheries. Instead, it has been exceptional DFO ministers, all from the Atlantic region, who have defended and promoted the industry.

In the late 1970s, Liberal DFO Minister Roméo LeBlanc from Acadian New Brunswick brought in the 200-mile limit to exclude foreign fleets, led in establishing the International Law of the Sea, and implemented the Fleet Separation Policy. Progressive Conservative minister John Crosbie and Liberal Brian Tobin, both from Newfoundland and Labrador, shut down the groundfish fisheries when stocks collapsed in the 1990s and won Cabinet support for large-scale adjustment programs to sustain the fishing labour force and fishing communities through the crisis. In 2008, Conservative DFO minister Gail Shea from Prince Edward Island brought in the Preserving the Independence of the Inshore Fleet in Canada's Atlantic Fisheries Policy (PIIFCAF) to strengthen enforcement of the Owner-Operator and Fleet Separation Policies. And in 2018, Roméo LeBlanc's son, Dominic, created the Atlantic Fisheries Fund and introduced major changes to the Fisheries Act to give Fleet Separation, Owner-Operator, and PIIFCAF Policies the force of law. The discouraging aspect of this history, however, is that these ministers have too often had to overcome inertia in the department and resistance from central agencies and at the Cabinet table to solve problems and move the industry forward.

The fishery is critically important to the economies of the Atlantic provinces and other fishing regions in the North and West of Canada, and it offers huge potential for development and reconciliation for Indigenous peoples. This book surveys convincing evidence that imminent demographic and labour market challenges put these many social, economic, and cultural contributions of the fishery at risk. But the question has to be asked: Will the federal government provide the leadership and invest the political and fiscal capital needed to meet these challenges? More basically, will a crisis in the fisheries in Atlantic Canada and in other rural coastal regions of the country register on the political barometers in Ottawa and on the national media seismographs in Toronto and Montreal?

There is one additional perspective I bring to this discussion that I should explain. Throughout the book, I look at the fishery primarily as an economic sector supporting jobs and incomes in coastal communities and contributing to economic development in disadvantaged regions and for Indigenous populations. While it goes without saying that commercial fisheries depend on healthy marine ecosystems, many readers—particularly those who are active on environmental issues—may find my primary focus on economics and social factors frustrating. They may challenge my lack of attention to the critical issue of whether fish populations are healthy enough today to sustain current levels of exploitation, let alone support growth in future.

I recognize and respect these concerns. I am not a fisheries scientist or an oceanographer and I lack the expertise to even attempt to predict sustainable harvesting levels for fish stocks into the future. Quite honestly, I rely on experience and historical perspective rather than science to make the case that the fishery is an important source of future social and economic development.

When I first started working with fish harvesters in the mid-1970s, the crisis that was bringing new harvester organizations to life across the entire Atlantic region was the rapacious exploitation of groundfish stocks by foreign dragger fleets operating within 12 miles of our coasts. After the 200-mile limit excluded foreign fishing fleets in 1977, federal and provincial governments invested heavily to build up a Canadian offshore industry on the same industrial template. Inshore harvesters were mobilizing to defend their own economic interests, but also to challenge government policies centred on big companies and industrial fleets pumping low-value products into global commodity markets.

For me, fish harvesters were the little guys fighting for their livelihoods and communities, but also to protect fish stocks from a large-scale corporate-industrial model that was fundamentally incompatible with a wild animal harvest. Although the fishery and the people in it have changed dramatically, I see fish harvesters still fighting that same battle today.

I have worked with those emerging harvester organizations—the Maritime Fishermen's Union, the Food, Fish and Allied Workers Union in Newfoundland and Labrador, the Prince Edward Island Fishermen's Association, the Alliance des pêcheurs professionnels du Québec, the United Fishermen and Allied Workers' Union, and the Native Brotherhood of British Columbia, among many others—since their origins and watched them evolve from a narrow focus on higher fish prices and getting larger shares of allowable catches to being full and effective partners in managing fisheries within an ecosystem framework. We are today at a point in that evolution where the rebuilding and enhanced conservation of fish stocks would not be possible without the leadership, organizational capacities, and knowledge resources of harvester organizations and their leaders. While still learning and still struggling with conflicting interests—and sometimes with each other—fish harvesters today serve as the primary stewards of fish stocks and habitats as much as they are users of those resources.

Quite frankly, I believe environmental organizations make profound errors, strategically and ethically, when they characterize fish harvesters as their opponents in debates over fisheries conservation and stock rebuilding. They are making enemies of people who have the greatest material interest in resource sustainability and who are potential partners and allies in protecting marine ecosystems, especially with the looming threat of climate change. There certainly are irresponsible individuals in the fish harvesting sector, just as there are in any other industry, but the most important distinction to make is that between harvesters, whose futures depend on healthy fish stocks, and other industry players who don't share the same long-term vested interests.

The other perspective I bring to this discussion is that, in the fishery, everything changes all the time. In the 1970s and early 1980s on the Atlantic coast, groundfish disappeared from inshore fishing grounds but herring and mackerel catches were stable, and lobster catches were up and down. In the 1990s, almost all groundfish stocks—cod, haddock, hake, red fish, halibut, etc.—collapsed to the point where a moratorium was imposed across the entire region and forty thousand people lost their jobs in harvesting and processing. Overfishing was definitely a primary cause, but climatic, oceanographic, and biological factors also contributed to the collapse.

The absence of groundfish predators likely contributed to the extraordinary growth of lobster, shrimp, and crab populations, and the fishery rebuilt itself around the harvest of shellfish. By the early 2000s, despite the groundfish shutdown, industry-wide landed values and export earnings were hitting all-time highs. And now today groundfish stocks are building back—cod on the northeast coast of Newfoundland, redfish in the Gulf of St. Lawrence and halibut everywhere—and, perhaps as a consequence, shrimp and snow crab populations are trending downwards in northeast regions. With climate change, lobster populations seem to be growing strongly in almost all eastern Canadian waters while they decline in southern New England.

In British Columbia the critical issue has always been salmon. In the 1990s, the industry was hammered on two sides: DFO introduced more stringent conservation measures and closures to protect endangered sub-stocks, and the rapid expansion of fish farm production drove market prices down sharply. Falling harvester incomes, new licensing rules, and reduced fishing opportunities led to government buyback programs that eventually halved the size of the overall fishing fleet. Today a much smaller industry carries on, buoyed by stable groundfish and shellfish landings and strong market prices for almost all products, including salmon. However, licensing policies in British Columbia do not support the sharing of this wealth as equitably as is the case in the Atlantic coast fishery (this issue is examined in greater depth in chapter 9).

The bottom-line argument I make in this book is that, even with the high risks arising from climate change, there will be a fishing industry in Canada over the next twenty-five to thirty years, and its products will grow in value as global consumer demand expands and freer trade opens up new markets. To generate economic growth in the fishery we do not have to catch more fish or put fish stocks under more pressure; we just have to produce high-quality products and get them to market. In fact, given new trade restrictions on illegal, unreported, and unregulated fisheries, and more stringent eco-labelling and traceability standards, the more sustainably we harvest our fish, the more its value in the market may grow.

This is not just a prediction about the future; it is a description of what has been happening for the past decade. Consider the macro-level information on Canadian fisheries on the next page in figure (a).

In 2009, with the fishery mired in the global recession, the industry produced 914,033 metric tonnes of fish and revenues of $1.9 billion for harvesting enterprises (i.e., "landed value"), and total seafood exports were valued at $3.7 billion.[3] In 2018, the Canadian fishing industry landed 12% fewer tonnes of fish than in 2009, but the harvesting sector saw landed values up by 98%, and the value of exports increased by 67% over the period in after-inflation dollars. It may seem too simple, but the industry should not need to catch more fish or threaten stock health to generate more wealth. We just need to manage what we have sustainably and get it to the right markets.

Again, experience shows that everything changes in the fishery, all the time. The mix of fish landings will keep changing with groundfish up and shellfish down in some areas, and perhaps the reverse in

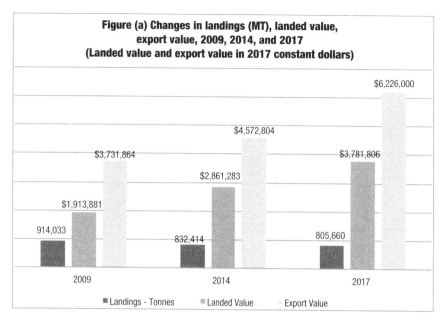

Figure (a) Changes in landings (MT), landed value, export value, 2009, 2014, and 2017 (Landed value and export value in 2017 constant dollars)

	2009	2014	2017
Landings - Tonnes	914,033	832,414	805,660
Landed Value	$1,913,881	$2,861,283	$3,781,806
Export Value	$3,731,864	$4,572,804	$6,226,000

others. In British Columbia, there may be big runs of salmon or herring in one year and empty nets the next. In the current global trade environment, we cannot be certain of future access to booming seafood markets in China or Europe, but those billions of people have to eat, and more consumers at home and abroad will continue choosing seafood for health reasons. There are credible disaster scenarios—tariff wars, military conflicts, new animal diseases, and more rapid climate change than anticipated. We have to manage these risks and hedge our bets, but we also have to deal with the here-and-now situations and the opportunities before us. The fishery won't go away, and we should make the most of it with responsible, sustainable management and fair treatment of the people who work in it.

It is my hope that this book will contribute to a heightened awareness of these issues, of the importance of the fish harvesting industry, and of its potential to make ever-greater contributions in future.

LIST OF ABBREVIATIONS

CCPFH: Canadian Council of Professional Fish Harvesters

CETA: Comprehensive Economic and Trade Agreement

CIFHF: Canadian Independent Fish Harvesters Federation

CMAS: Census Metropolitan Areas

COPS: Canadian Occupational Projection System

DFO: Department of Fisheries and Oceans

EI: Employment Insurance

FFAW: Unifor Fish, Food and Allied Workers Union

FLMI: Fisheries Labour Market Information Study

SCOFO: Standing Committee on Fisheries and Oceans (House of Commons)

ISED: Department of Innovation, Science and Economic Development

ITQS: individual transferable quotas

LMI: Labour Market Information

MSC: Marine Stewardship Council

NAICS: North American Industry Classification System

OECD: Organisation for Economic Co-operation and Development

OP: occupational pluralism

PIIFCAF: Preserving the Independence of the Inshore Fleet in Canada's Atlantic Fisheries

TAC: total allowable catch

UI: Unemployment Insurance

VER: regionally variable entrance requirements

Chapter 1

AN EMERGING CRISIS

This book is based in large part on findings and policy advice developed by the Fisheries Labour Market Information Study (FLMI), a three-year national research and consultation project completed in 2018 by the Canadian Council of Professional Fish Harvesters (CCPFH). I was the project leader for the FLMI and currently serve as Research Director for the CCPFH.

The CCPFH, the national human resources sector council for the Canadian fish harvesting industry, is governed by a board of directors drawn from organizations representing captains and crew in Atlantic, Pacific, freshwater, and Indigenous fisheries. Founded in 1995, the CCPFH's main objective is to ensure that Canada's fish harvesting industry has the leadership and resources needed to respond to changing labour supply conditions, and that fish harvesters themselves have the knowledge and skills required to work safely and advance in their profession. The council undertakes research and strategic planning projects and develops and disseminates education and training tools to address priorities set out by industry stakeholders.

In 2005, the CCPFH completed a study of labour supply trends in the Canadian fish harvesting industry. The report identified an emerging crisis driven by demographic trends, low incomes, and shrinking employment opportunities in the industry.[4] With the average age for fishing captains in their early fifties, and crew workers in their forties, a third or more of the harvesting labour force would age out of the industry within ten years. And with stagnant incomes and uncertain career prospects, most fishing fleets were not well positioned to attract and retain new entrants to replace retirees.

By 2015, there was growing recognition that the labour supply crisis anticipated by the 2005 CCPFH study was well advanced. Fish processing plants in Atlantic Canada were becoming heavily dependent on temporary foreign workers, and fishing fleets were finding it increasingly difficult to find crew workers. There was growing risk that the number of fishing enterprises in some regions could shrink significantly—not because there were no fish to catch or markets to sell to, but due to shortages of skilled people to operate vessels and, most importantly, take over enterprises from retiring owner-operators.

In response, the CCPFH initiated the FLMI study to update the 2005 analysis and to explore ways to rebuild the labour force by making fisheries employment more attractive and rewarding. There was a specific focus on the role of *occupational pluralism*—fish harvesters working in other industries outside the fishing season to supplement incomes and raise capital to invest in their fishing enterprises—in sustaining the labour supply in different fishing regions and fleets.

It became evident early in the FLMI study that conditions were changing rapidly. Most strikingly, the industry was undergoing a dramatic economic turnaround compared to the early 2000s. Landed values for many seafood products were rising in response to global market demand, and after two decades of shrinkage, the decline in the numbers of fishing enterprises and fish harvesting jobs was levelling off. As well, harvester incomes were trending up.

There were also indications that with greater numbers of owner-operators reaching retirement age, the market for access rights was increasingly volatile. Rising demand for seafood products was pushing up the market value of fishing licences and quotas, creating new barriers to intergenerational transfers within fishing families and communities. Access to affordable credit was increasingly difficult for younger harvesters seeking to become enterprise owners.

Responding to these emerging realities and their impacts in re-shaping the fish harvesting industry in different parts of Canada, the final report for the CCPFH's FLMI study, *Fisheries Seasonality and the Allocation of Labour and Skills Labour Market Information,*[5] identifies three high-priority areas for intervention by industry and community leaders and government agencies: enhancing the economic viability and labour market competitiveness of fishing fleets; facilitating intergenerational transfer of fishing assets; and attracting and retaining new labour supply.

The following chapters summarize the major findings from the CCPFH report and explore strategies to address these change and development priorities.

Chapter 2

THE FISHERY

Driving Economic Renewal
in Rural Coastal Communities

I n 2017, *federal finance minister Bill Morneau's Advisory Council on* Economic Growth, chaired by Dominic Barton, released a series of reports providing "advice on concrete policy actions to help create the conditions for strong and sustained long-term economic growth."[6] The second report, titled *Unleashing the Growth Potential of Key Sectors*, promoted strategies for expanding exports and targeted eight "high potential sectors" where "Canada has a strong endowment, untapped potential, and significant global growth prospects." The first of these eight sectors was "agfood," encompassing the full range of products from the agriculture, fisheries, and aquaculture industries.

> *Booming demand for food and an expanding global middle class should benefit Canada's agfood sector significantly. By 2050, global demand is expected to rise by 70 percent....A good deal of this demand will come from emerging markets, where some three billion people are expected to enter the middle class from 2010 to 2030—particularly in Asia—and to*

consume considerably more protein than their less wealthy counterparts do today. Many middle-class consumers also want proof that their food has been produced in a safe and environmentally sustainable way. Our potential [agfood] output greatly exceeds the requirements of the population, so this country could become an increasingly significant source of high-quality food to feed the world's growing middle class, while ensuring accessibility to affordable, nutritious, and healthy food at home.[7]

The report does not mention wild-caught fisheries, but the analysis applies directly to the seafood sector and helps explain the growth trends in the industry since the end of the Great Recession (2007–2009).

SEAFOOD EXPORTS

According to Industry Canada trade data, seafood exports reached $6.2 billion in value in 2017, a 65% increase in constant dollar (i.e., after-inflation) value over 2009 (figure 2.1).[8] Exports from the entire agfood sector, to which seafood contributes about 10%, grew by just 46% over the period.

Along with efforts to expand exports through more aggressive marketing and new trade agreements, there is also a policy push to diversify markets to reduce Canada's long-standing dependence on one dominant trading partner, the United States. As figure 2.2 illustrates, the 2009 to 2017 period saw growth in the value of seafood shipments to every major regional market.

The United States is still dominant, but seafood exports to China are expanding rapidly, approaching $1 billion in 2017, while shipments to other regions, including Eastern Europe and Latin America, are also showing new strength. This has all been happening

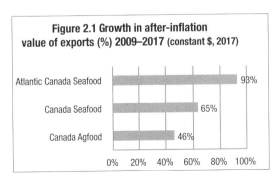

Figure 2.1 Growth in after-inflation value of exports (%) 2009–2017 (constant $, 2017)

Atlantic Canada Seafood — 93%
Canada Seafood — 65%
Canada Agfood — 46%

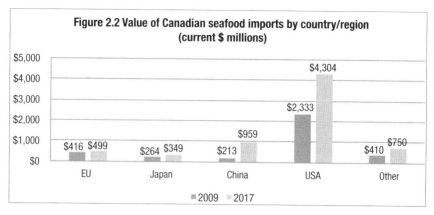

Figure 2.2 Value of Canadian seafood imports by country/region (current $ millions)

	EU	Japan	China	USA	Other
2009	$416	$264	$213	$2,333	$410
2017	$499	$349	$959	$4,304	$750

prior to the full implementation of the Comprehensive Economic and Trade Agreement (CETA) with the European Union and new trade arrangements with Pacific Rim countries.

And as figure 2.3 indicates, Canadian seafood exporters are now reaching consumers in European and Asian nations who eat more seafood than is generally the case in our traditional markets.[9]

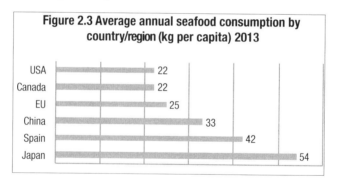

Figure 2.3 Average annual seafood consumption by country/region (kg per capita) 2013

USA	22
Canada	22
EU	25
China	33
Spain	42
Japan	54

It's particularly noteworthy that the new wealth generated by increasing fisheries exports is impacting provinces and rural coastal regions most in need of economic renewal. The fishery is the leading export sector in Nova Scotia and a top performer in the other Atlantic provinces. Most importantly, seafood is outpacing other industry sectors in export growth. In five of the six Canadian provinces with substantial commercial fisheries, the after-inflation value of international seafood shipments grew at much higher rates than total exports from all industry sectors (table 2.1).

TABLE 2.1. GROWTH IN THE VALUE OF SEAFOOD EXPORTS 2009–2017 (CONSTANT 2017 $ MILLIONS)

	Seafood Exports 2009	Seafood Exports 2017	% Growth Seafood Exports	% Growth Total Exports, All Sectors
Newfoundland and Labrador	$568	$898	58%	3%
Prince Edward Island	$144	$208	45%	14%
Nova Scotia	$887	$1,843	108%	11%
New Brunswick	$646	$1,384	114%	53%
Quebec	$178	$396	122%	28%
British Columbia[10]	$991	$1,273	28%	51%
Canada	$3,786	$6,226	64%	16%

FIXED SUPPLY MEETS EXPLODING DEMAND

On the surface, the growth in Canadian seafood exports is easy to describe and perhaps downplay as a short-term or cyclical trend that can easily fade away. The American and European economies bounced back after the Great Recession, and exchange rates have been favourable for Canadian exporters, but all that can change, as we have seen over the past two decades. And while seafood exports to Asia are currently surging, current trade disputes and political tensions suggest we should not take for granted future access to these markets.

On a deeper level, however, there are solid reasons to anticipate a medium- to long-term future of sustained growth in the Canadian fishing industry. The key factors to consider are resource supplies and market demand. Thirty years ago, the Canadian fishing industry was a volume-driven sector, pumping overabundant commodities into buyers' markets. Today's industry is reshaping itself to produce higher value products in an environment of strengthening market demand. The rising tide has not reached all boats, and not all industry sectors are taking full advantage of the new opportunities; however, it is time to substantially revise our thinking about the fishery and its current and future economic contributions.

On the resource side, the harvesting of most commercially important fish stocks is now managed at sustainable levels within ecosystem-based and precautionary approaches. With recent federal funding increases for fisheries science, strengthened habitat protections in a newly revised Fisheries Act, requirements for catch monitoring at-sea and at-landing sites in most fisheries, and designation of new marine protected areas, there is no reason to anticipate weaker commitments to resource and habitat protection by government and industry. Climate change and other marine environmental factors are certainly impacting Pacific salmon and are likely affecting the current rebalancing of shellfish and groundfish populations on the Atlantic coast. We should therefore expect the mix of fishing activities to continue to change, with good and bad years for different fleets and regions, but there are now few instances in Canadian fisheries where chronic overfishing is, in and of itself, a major threat to stock sustainability.

Perhaps most importantly, fish harvester leaders and their organizations increasingly understand that future growth in enterprise profitability will come much more from improving product values than from landing more fish. The most successful harvesters will be the ones delivering the highest quality fish at the right times of the year to processors with access to the most lucrative markets. With the growing influence of international conservation standards, such as Marine Stewardship Council (MSC) certification, and new traceability requirements to prevent illegal, unreported, and unregulated fisheries, industry leaders also know they have to be responsible stewards of resources if they are to maintain access to markets and higher prices for their fish.

On the market side, barring major trade disruptions or military conflicts, global demand for seafood has nowhere to go but up, and exports will remain the driving force in the Canadian fishing economy. It's a simple formula, as figure 2.4 shows: within sustainably managed fisheries, catch volumes and the supply of wild-caught fish to the market will grow very little over time while more and more consumers will want more and more seafood. In this environment, the value of our exports can only keep going up.

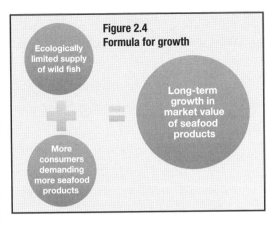

Figure 2.4
Formula for growth

Fisheries and Oceans Canada, generally known as DFO, provides fisheries landings and exports data that reveal how exports impact the landed value of fish products, i.e., the gross revenues to fish harvesters when they sell their catch at the plant gate.[11]

In figure 2.5, total fish landings (in metric tonnes) and landed value and export earnings adjusted for inflation are indexed to the year 2000 for all Canadian fisheries to show percentage changes on a year-to-year basis from 2000 to 2017.[12] The industry's vulnerability to shifts and shocks in the global economy is evident, as is the way in which landed values closely track export values. From 2000 to 2009,

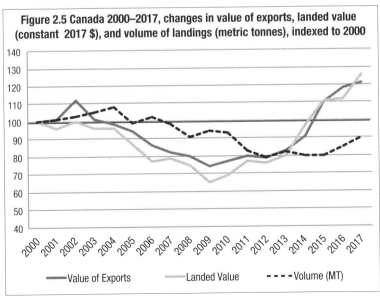

Figure 2.5 Canada 2000–2017, changes in value of exports, landed value (constant 2017 $), and volume of landings (metric tonnes), indexed to 2000

Value of Exports ——— Landed Value ——— Volume (MT) - - - -

the Canadian dollar was near par with the US dollar for a period, followed by the global economic recession, and under these stresses both exports and revenues to harvesters lost up to one-third of after-inflation value. However, from 2009 to 2017, the value of Canadian seafood exports rebounded by 64%, and landed values grew by 94% in constant dollar terms.

The dotted line in figure 2.5 shows changes in the volume in metric tonnes of reported fish landings. The important point to note is the limited extent to which the amount of fish caught and brought to market determines the revenues generated. Over the 2000–2009 period, landed values and export earnings fell off much more sharply than landed volumes, meaning that seafood products were selling for progressively lower prices in global markets. However, the dramatic rise in export earnings and landed values after 2009 occurred despite flat production levels. In short, the rising economic contribution of fisheries is not a consequence of higher landings and greater pressure on fish stocks, but instead it reflects the impacts of accelerating market demand on product values.

In discussions about the fishery, it is often suggested that the current industry surge is largely the result of booming lobster landings and sales and is not reflective of conditions across the entire industry. Lobster is certainly the dominant sector in Canadian fisheries at present, as is evident from the landed volume and value numbers in table 2.2.

TABLE 2.2 LANDED VOLUMES (METRIC TONNES) AND VALUES ($ MILLIONS) OF MAJOR COMMERCIAL FISHERIES, 2017

	Catch Volume (MT)	Landed Value ($ millions)
Atlantic Lobster	97,452	$1,462
Atlantic Snow Crab	92,458	$968
Atlantic Groundfish	93,866	$227
British Columbia Groundfish	129,645	$175
British Columbia Shellfish	12,120	$143
British Columbia Salmon	12,893	$46

However, the reality of the industry is more complex and much more interesting. Figure 2.6 compares 2009 and 2017 in terms of the constant dollar value and volume, in metric tonnes, of landings in the shellfish,[13] salmon, and groundfish fisheries in British Columbia and in the groundfish, snow crab, and lobster fisheries in the Atlantic provinces and Quebec.

This data confirms that the economic contributions of all major commercial fisheries improved over the 2009–2017 period, in some cases in spite of weak or declining landings. Only Atlantic lobster and British Columbia groundfish show significant increases in both volumes and landed values, while values went up as landings remained stable or declined in the other fisheries.

Dividing the total landed value for each species by the number of metric tonnes landed gives the ratio of landed volume to landed value. Figure 2.7 shows percentage changes in these ratios in 2017 over 2009.

On a value per tonne basis, growth in after-inflation market value is consistent across all major commercial fisheries, with salmon on the west coast and snow crab in Atlantic Canada outpacing lobster.

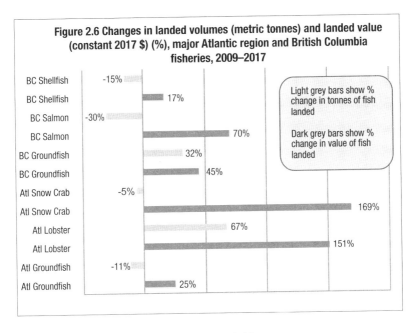

Figure 2.6 Changes in landed volumes (metric tonnes) and landed value (constant 2017 $) (%), major Atlantic region and British Columbia fisheries, 2009–2017

It is important to bear in mind that the ups and downs in fish landings do not necessarily mean that fish stocks are in trouble or that fleets are increasing fishing effort and risking sustainability. DFO fisheries plans constantly revise allowable catch levels to manage natural cycles in stock abundance and other factors. For example, reduced salmon landings in British Columbia often result from management decisions to close an entire fishery on a major river system to protect small sub-stocks that are under stress.

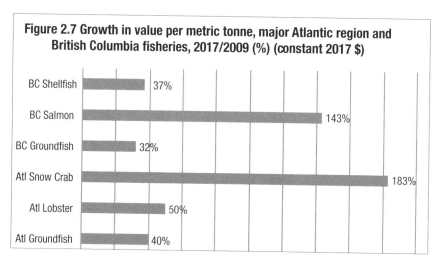

Figure 2.7 Growth in value per metric tonne, major Atlantic region and British Columbia fisheries, 2017/2009 (%) (constant 2017 $)

- BC Shellfish — 37%
- BC Salmon — 143%
- BC Groundfish — 32%
- Atl Snow Crab — 183%
- Atl Lobster — 50%
- Atl Groundfish — 40%

The rise in lobster landings may stem in part from warming water temperatures due to climate change but is also a return on decades of investment by the industry in aggressive conservation measures, including increased carapace size limits to catch larger animals, not harvesting females, escape hatches to allow juveniles to exit traps, and mechanisms to prevent ghost fishing (i.e., traps lost in storms continuing to catch and kill lobster). In the Gulf of St. Lawrence, the Maritime Fishermen's Union has been constructing artificial reefs and seeding larvae to build up local lobster populations. In the groundfish industry, a solid recovery of the northern cod stocks is underway in Newfoundland and Labrador and industry and DFO scientists are working together to ensure that catch levels do not jeopardize long-term rebuilding in both inshore and offshore areas.

(CCPFH)

Put quite simply, the large-scale harvest of wild fish populations is always going to be a dynamic learning process requiring constant adjustments in fishing effort, methods, and controls, but the foundations for long-term sustainability—improving fisheries data, science-driven stock assessment, and industry-government collaboration—are largely in place for most important commercial fisheries in Canadian waters. More serious challenges often arise with fish stocks that migrate through international waters, such as salmon, mackerel, and bluefin tuna off the Atlantic coast, and the major salmon stocks in the Pacific.

In summary, strong growth in market demand is creating conditions for harvesting and processing enterprises in many fisheries to thrive with or without increasing landings. It should therefore be possible to grow the economic benefits generated from fisheries without ramping up pressure on vulnerable fish stocks. There will be ups and downs, but there are solid reasons to manage fisheries and promote the industry on the assumption that the trends since 2009 are reasonably predictive of the foreseeable future.

THE BIG QUESTION

The big question raised by this outlook is, who will benefit from the future growth in the value of seafood products? From a labour market perspective, industry growth promises both opportunity and risk. The major opportunity is that, with stronger revenues, fish harvesting enterprises will be better positioned to compete for new labour supply, drawing young people to careers in the industry and helping to repopulate and revitalize rural coastal communities. As well, with improving business viability, new entrants should find it easier to access investment capital to take ownership of fishing enterprises from retiring harvesters.

But there are downside risks. Growing market demand for seafood holds some potential to undermine long-term efforts to protect vulnerable fish stocks by expanding the economic incentives for harvesting and processing enterprises to irresponsibly intensify production levels. This risk is particularly acute in fisheries where licence and quota prices have risen precipitously, and new entrant harvesters take on excessive debt burdens to buy into the fishery.

As the fish in the water become more valuable, the rights to catch and process them will also grow in value. More and more investors, beyond the harvesters who make their living from fishing, will want to gain ownership or control of fishing licences and quotas as speculative investments, as sources of rentier incomes, or as more secure sources of raw material for vertically integrated businesses. Over the past decade, we have seen more investors from outside the industry, and sometimes from outside Canada, buying up fishing access rights in anticipation of their future market value. In British Columbia, DFO policies allow such owner-investors to lease out licences and quotas to active fish harvesters as a source of rental revenues. Fish processing companies in all regions have been increasingly aggressive in their efforts to control and expand raw material supplies for their plants, and this also has contributed to inflation in market prices for access rights.

Over time, a continuing loss of harvester ownership and control of licences and quotas could transfer an ever-greater share of the new wealth the industry is generating away from fishing communities and adjacent coastal regions. In Atlantic Canada successive DFO ministers have taken strong stands to avoid such outcomes. A 2007 policy document titled *Preserving the Independence of the Inshore Fleet in Canada's Atlantic Fisheries* (PIIFCAF) identified two foundational policies and defined their purpose very clearly: "The fleet separation policy, established in 1979, and the owner-operator policy, established in 1989, are part of a suite of policy initiatives designed to support an independent inshore fleet in Atlantic Canada—with the wealth and value flowing from the licences held and controlled by individual fishermen remaining in their communities across Atlantic Canada."[14]

The Honourable Roméo LeBlanc from New Brunswick introduced the Fleet Separation Policy with the specific goal of assuring an economic base for fishing communities in Atlantic Canada and Quebec. The policy established that only active fish harvesters, and not fish processing companies, could own licences and quotas in fleets comprised of vessels sixty-five feet in length or less. In 1989, Progressive Conservative fisheries minister Tom Siddon approved the Owner-Operator Policy, again only for Atlantic inshore fisheries, to require enterprise owners to actively fish their licences or quotas and not lease them out or pay someone else to fish for them. In 2008, Minister Gail Shea in the Harper Conservative government announced PIIFCAF as a means to strengthen enforcement of both of these policies.

In 2016, Liberal DFO minister Dominic LeBlanc initiated steps to embed the Owner-Operator and Fleet Separation Policies in legislation and regulations to give them clearer legal status and permanence. In a speech to industry organizations in 2017, he set out his objectives:

The Owner-Operator, Fleet Separation and PIIFCAF policies exist to ensure that inshore and midshore harvesters remain independent, and that the benefits of inshore and midshore fishing licenses flow to the fish harvesters who hold them and to the coastal communities that depend on the resource. These policies are helping to generate stable and long-term economic prosperity in Atlantic Canada and they're helping the middle class thrive.…

With this review of the Fisheries Act, I also have the opportunity to make amendments to the Act that will strengthen fish management policies, and I intend to use this opportunity to enshrine owner-operator and fleet separation in law. This will mean a legislative framework that affirms the ability of the Fisheries Minister to consider social and economic objectives in administering the Fisheries Act.[15]

Under DFO minister Jonathan Wilkinson, the new Fisheries Act was passed into law in June 2019, and supportive regulations are being finalized at time of writing. It is an open and active question as to whether and how the commitment in the revised Fisheries Act to pursue social and economic objectives through fisheries licensing policies and management plans will be applied in British Columbia where the Owner-Operator and Fleet Separation Policies have never been in place.

In the following chapters, the strategic focus will be on ways to leverage anticipated industry growth to address pressing labour market challenges—challenges that arguably jeopardize the policy objectives of successive fisheries ministers to sustain independent fishing enterprises and rural coastal communities. We can point to other primary production industries where economic expansion resulted in the displacement of small-scale producers and the marginalization and depopulation of their communities. The fishery is now on a path to growth, a small but important niche sector that is expanding its value more rapidly than almost any other because of exploding global demand for its products and their value to human health and well-being. The decision and actions of governments and industry leaders over the next decade will determine who benefits from this growth and whether this industry can navigate a different course toward sustainability for both the resource base and the adjacent rural coastal communities that depend on it.

Chapter 3

ENOUGH FISH, NOT ENOUGH FISH HARVESTERS

*T*hrough the 1990s and into the 2000s, if you asked any fisheries expert to describe the state of the industry, you'd likely get the simple answer, "Too many fishermen, not enough fish." This response seemed sufficient at the time to avoid having to dig deeper into complex and rapidly changing social, economic, and ecological conditions.

RIGHT-SIZING GONE WRONG

In the 1990s, the collapse of Atlantic groundfish stocks displaced thousands of harvesters and plant workers, and severe stock fluctuations and market shifts destabilized the British Columbia salmon fishery. Federal and provincial governments on both coasts shared the view that industry overcapacity and "too many fishermen" were threats to vulnerable fish stocks and a serious constraint on enterprise viability, particularly in owner-operated small-boat fleets. The consensus among most policy-makers was that fishing fleets had to downsize, and people in coastal communities needed to look elsewhere for employment and incomes.

And the message took hold. Young people in fishing regions stayed in school longer to have more career options. Many then left for jobs in regional urban centres or, from the Atlantic region, headed west in search of employment in the booming oil and gas industry. They were often encouraged to leave by parents who worked in fisheries but saw no future there. In a 2004 CCPFH survey of fishing captains and crew, 40% of respondents in the Atlantic region and over 60% in British Columbia reported that if a young person asked their advice they would discourage them from pursuing careers in fishing.[16]

In the mid-1990s, the federal government invested over $2 billion to "adjust" people out of the industry on both coasts through licence buybacks, early retirement incentives, and vocational training programs. The 1990–2017 period saw an almost 50% reduction in registered fishing vessels in Atlantic Canada and 60% in British Columbia (figure 3.1).[17]

Fleet downsizing of course meant workforce downsizing. As will be discussed in greater detail in the next chapter, Canada Census data suggests that from 1991 to 2016 the number of Canadians who identified fishing as their primary occupation shrank by one-third.

This raises a critical issue: how far can we go with downsizing a widely dispersed rural industry before we reach a point of no return? If the number of people working in a rural labour force declines significantly over a short time period, will disruptions in family and community situations start to accelerate workforce shrinkage to the point where it can't be controlled or reversed?

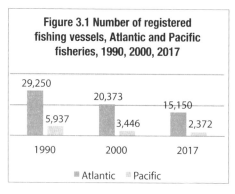

Figure 3.1 Number of registered fishing vessels, Atlantic and Pacific fisheries, 1990, 2000, 2017

29,250

20,373

15,150

5,937

3,446

2,372

1990   2000   2017

■ Atlantic ■ Pacific

Fisheries managers and scientists have perhaps done a good job matching up the numbers of fishing vessels and their catching capacities with available fish stocks to achieve sustainable harvesting levels, but how much thought has gone into the human side of the equation? Sustaining a labour force in a geographically anchored industry requires successive generations of workers. Workers come with families, and families require services and amenities more or less comparable with what's available in more urban settings. Efficient provision of services and amenities requires people to live in communities, and communities require certain numbers of service users and taxpayers to remain viable. For families to commit to pursuing their lives in fishing communities there has to be a sense of security for current and future generations.

In short, the process of "right-sizing" the fishing industry involves more than matching up fishing boats and gear with available fish stocks. The compelling issue that arises from this research is that decision-makers have given inadequate policy attention to what's needed to sustain a labour force that can maintain the industry. This lack of foresight and proactive policy work is now bringing the industry to the brink of crisis.

THE RURAL DEMOGRAPHIC CHALLENGE

It is important to consider looming labour supply challenges in the fishing industry against the background of an emerging population crisis in rural Canada. A definitive overview of population trends in rural Canada is provided in a report by an eminent expert on rural population dynamics, Ray Bollman, for the Federation of Canadian Municipalities.[18] Bollman begins by defining two urban and rural "geographies" for Canada.

The urban Census Metropolitan Areas (CMAs) are defined by Statistics Canada as cities with populations of 100,000 or more, together with neighbouring towns or municipalities where 50% or more of the resident workforce commutes to the core urban area. The rural geography is made up of all other Census Divisions outside CMAs.

In 2011, 23 million Canadians (69% of the total population) lived in urban-metropolitan regions while 10 million (31%) lived in rural regions comprised of smaller cities, towns, unincorporated communities, and other less populated areas.[19]

Differentiating urban and rural regions in this way, Ray Bollman's report identified the contributions of Canada's rural regions to population and economy as measured by gross domestic product (GDP). The findings for seven provinces with significant fishing industries and for Canada, excluding the northern territories, are shown in table 3.1.

TABLE 3.1 RURAL CONTRIBUTIONS TO POPULATION AND ECONOMY, 2011 (%)		
	% of Total Population	% of Total Industry GDP
Newfoundland and Labrador	61	61
Prince Edward Island	100	100
Nova Scotia	56	50
New Brunswick	64	63
Quebec	31	30
Manitoba	39	35
British Columbia	31	32
Canada excluding 3 northern territories	31	30

The report found that rural regions, as Bollman defines them, sustain 31% of Canada's population and contribute 43% of GDP from goods production, 24% of GDP from services, and 28% of total employment in Canada.[20] These findings would suggest that rural population decline represents a potentially serious threat to the stability of the Canadian economy overall.

The Federation of Canadian Municipalities report examines trends for three components of population change: natural balance (births and deaths), domestic or in-country migration, and international migration. For the first of these, it projected that Canada will have more deaths than births by 2030, after which the population can only grow by international migration. However, this deflection point has already been reached in many parts of rural Canada. Over the 1996–2012 period, 29 rural Census Divisions experienced more deaths than births, 10 of them in fisheries-dependent regions in the Maritimes and Quebec.

Regarding internal migration, 43 rural Census Divisions experienced net population loss in each year from 1996 to 2012, 15 of them with significant fisheries in Atlantic Canada and British Columbia. And only a handful of rural Census Divisions, almost all in Alberta and Saskatchewan, made population gains through international migration over the same period.

Perhaps the most compelling evidence on the demographic challenges facing rural Canada is the changing age composition and the falling numbers of young people in many rural regions. Table 3.2 describes the ratio of potential labour market new entrants to potential retirees in 2012.[21]

TABLE 3.2 POTENTIAL LABOUR MARKET ENTRANTS (10–19 YEARS OF AGE) IN 2012 AS A PERCENTAGE OF THE NUMBER OF POTENTIAL RETIREES (55–64 YEARS OF AGE)		
	Urban CMAs (%)	Rural Census Divisions (%)
Newfoundland and Labrador	79	63
Prince Edward Island	(No CMA)	88
Nova Scotia	80	75
New Brunswick	83	70
Quebec	85	70
Ontario	101	81
Manitoba	100	122
Saskatchewan	107	105
Alberta	100	111
British Columbia	86	73
Canada	94	81

While some urban areas also face demographic challenges, the outlook in many rural regions is stark. Without significant gains from interprovincial and international migration—where most rural regions are not currently performing well—critical labour shortages in strategically important rural industries are imminent and inescapable. Leaving aside any new job creation, this data suggests that 25–35% of job vacancies caused by retirements could go unfilled in many rural regions. The exceptions may be in the three Prairie provinces, a result of their substantial and growing Indigenous populations, along with the labour-drawing power of the oil and gas industry.

In his conclusions to the Federation of Canadian Municipalities report, Ray Bollman calls for a profound shift in thinking on rural social and economic development. He writes, "It appears that 'people-creation,' not job creation, holds the key to growth in rural Canada. Canada is approaching a scenario with more deaths than births—and many rural areas are already experiencing this scenario. To grow, migrants must be attracted from other areas of Canada or international immigrants must be attracted."[22]

From this perspective, Bollman suggests that economic development in the conventional sense is not the greatest need in many rural regions. With more and more employment opportunities becoming available as older workers retire, other interventions will be needed to generate internal and international migration flows that favour rural communities. Bollman prioritizes capacity building and strengthening of local governance so that communities can adapt to and lead the economic, social, and cultural changes that will be needed.

CHANGING AGE PROFILE OF FISH HARVESTER LABOUR FORCE

If rural regions and industries in general face demographic challenges, the outlook for more remote fisheries-dependent regions may be more daunting. Data from the 2001 and 2016 Census of Canada Household Surveys provides evidence of the demographic challenges facing the fishing industry. Figure 3.2 compares changes in the proportional sizes of four age groups for the general working-age population (all occupations) and the census occupational group "fishermen/women" in Canada.[23] The latter category includes fishing enterprise owner-operators and the majority of fishing crew.

In figure 3.2 the under-30 age group of fishermen/-women is a smaller proportion of the fisheries workforce than of the general population, and shrinks more over the 2001–2016 period, indicating a sharp fall-off in new entrants.[24] The 30–44 age group is critical to long-term stability and intergenerational labour force attachment in the fishing industry. Its decline from 41% to 28% of the fishing workforce suggests that significant numbers of young families left the industry and perhaps left fishing communities over the period.

The 45–54 age group saw an increase for fish harvesters and comprises a much greater share than in the general working population. In 2016, the over-54 age segment represented a smaller proportion of the fishing workforce than of the general labour force—understandable, given the more physically challenging nature of fisheries work—but this segment expanded more rapidly within fish harvesting than in the overall working population.

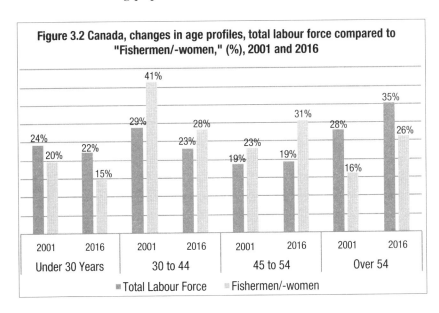

Figure 3.2 Canada, changes in age profiles, total labour force compared to "Fishermen/-women," (%), 2001 and 2016

(CCPFH)

It is important to note how much change occurred in just fifteen years in both the general working-age population and—more dramatically—the fisheries workforce.

The CCPFH FLMI study accessed data from Statistics Canada's tax filer system describing all individuals in Canada who reported $1,000 or more in income from fish harvesting employment over the

2000–2016 period. This data confirms findings from the census and adds more depth to our understanding of the issues.

Table 3.3 shows changes in the average age of employed fish harvesters by fishing province and for Canada from 2000 to 2016. Newfoundland and Labrador saw the most pronounced shift, beginning the period below the national average and ending 2 percentage points above it. Manitoba and British Columbia began the period with relatively older harvester workforces and maintained that status, while harvesters in the Maritimes were younger on average than in other provinces but trending in the same direction.

TABLE 3.3 AVERAGE AGE OF FISH HARVESTER TAX FILERS, 2000 AND 2016		
	2000	2016
Canada	40.8	46.7
Newfoundland and Labrador	39.9	48.7
Prince Edward Island	40.3	46.3
Nova Scotia	40.0	45.0
New Brunswick	41.0	45.4
Quebec	40.8	46.6
Manitoba	43.8	48.8
British Columbia	43.5	47.4

The tax filer data provides further insight into the internal shifts taking place in the fish harvesting labour force. Figures 3.2 to 3.5 show changes across five age cohorts over the 2000–2016 period for Canada overall and for three representative provinces. The fishing labour force in Nova Scotia has the youngest profile among all provinces, while harvesters in Newfoundland and Labrador and British Columbia have the oldest.

Important shifts are evident in all four figures. The first is the weak recruitment of young new entrants (<25 years of age) to the sector which again is most pronounced in Newfoundland and Labrador. This reflects both the lack of young people growing up in many coastal communities and the choices those present are making to pursue other careers.

Second, the core workforce of 25–44 years of age has declined in size in all regions—from half the harvester workforce in Canada in 2000 to less than a third in 2016. As noted above, this age group includes harvesters with young families who are key to the stability of their communities as well as to future labour supply and intergenerational succession in the ownership of fishing enterprises.

And third, the growing over-representation of harvesters at or past normal retirement age is a growing risk factor for the industry. For Canada as a whole, one-third of the harvesting labour force in 2016 was 55 years of age or older. Almost 40% of harvesters in both Newfoundland and Labrador and British Columbia were 55 years and older compared to 29% in Nova Scotia. Of particular note is the sharp

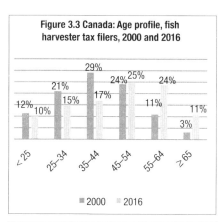

Figure 3.3 Canada: Age profile, fish harvester tax filers, 2000 and 2016

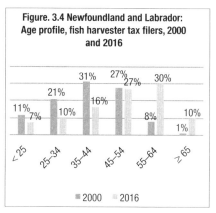

Figure. 3.4 Newfoundland and Labrador: Age profile, fish harvester tax filers, 2000 and 2016

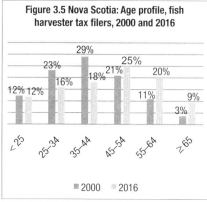

Figure 3.5 Nova Scotia: Age profile, fish harvester tax filers, 2000 and 2016

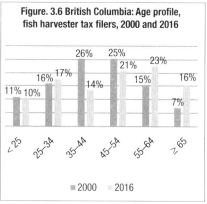

Figure. 3.6 British Columbia: Age profile, fish harvester tax filers, 2000 and 2016

increase in harvesters over the age of 64, up from 1% to 10% of the employed workforce in Newfoundland and Labrador, from 7% to 16% in British Columbia, and from 3% to 10% for Canada overall. In five provinces there was a higher percentage of working harvesters over the age of 64 than there was under the age of 25.

FEMALE PARTICIPATION

One interesting demographic change is the growing participation of women in the fish harvesting industry. Using tax filer data, table 3.4 shows changes over the 2000–2016 period in the percentage of individuals reporting fishing employment income who self-identified as female. There are marked differences among provinces in terms of female participation rates, whether they are increasing or not, and how much change took place over the period. Except for Manitoba, the provinces with relatively older harvester populations seem to also have higher rates of female participation, suggesting the possibility that the decline in the numbers of young male new entrants to the industry is creating more employment and career opportunities for women in the sector.

TABLE 3.4 PERCENTAGE OF FEMALE FISH HARVESTER TAX FILERS, 2000 AND 2016

	2000 (%)	2016 (%)
Newfoundland and Labrador	25.2	28.3
Prince Edward Island	23.4	26.0
Nova Scotia	15.1	15.5
New Brunswick	13.4	16.5
Quebec	18.6	16.3
Manitoba	11.9	17.2
British Columbia	26.2	25.5
Canada	20.7	21.2

LABOUR MOBILITY

In addition to demographic factors, the availability of new labour supply in the rural coastal regions of Canada has been constrained by intensified labour mobility at the regional and national levels over the past three decades. On average about 1.2 million Canadians have been moving permanently (i.e., changing their primary home addresses) each year over the past three decades. The majority (75%) relocate within a province or territory, while the remaining 25% are interprovincial migrants, moving from one province or territory to another.[25]

Since the 1990s, the dominant factor influencing interprovincial labour mobility in Canada has been economic expansion in western Canada. Employment growth in energy development, construction, transportation, and related fields has drawn working-age people away from the industries in eastern Canada that are less competitive on wages, salaries, and job security.

A report from the Centre for the Study of Living Standards provides a comprehensive overview of interprovincial migration in Canada.[26] Its analysis of trends over the 1987–2014 period identifies provincial gains and losses in the national labour market as shown in table 3.5.[27]

(CCPFH)

TABLE 3.5 NET INTERPROVINCIAL MIGRATION BY PROVINCE

Net interprovincial migration 1987–2014 (persons)									
QC	MB	SK	NL	ON	NB	NS	PE	BC	AB
-255,944	-141,378	-134,642	-85,597	-57,808	-35,640	-35,609	-3,072	+331,083	+433,851

Net interprovincial migration 1987–2014 as a percentage of 2014 population									
NL	SK	MB	NB	NS	QC	PE	ON	BC	AB
-16.2%	-12.0%	-11.0%	-4.7%	-3.8%	-3.1%	-2.1%	-0.4%	7.2%	10.5%

With the exception of British Columbia, provinces with significant fishing industries have been net exporters of population over the 1987–2014 period.

Newfoundland and Labrador had a net loss of almost 86,000 people through interprovincial migration, equivalent to 16% of its 2014 population.

The Maritime provinces together experienced net losses of more than 74,000 people, ranging from 2.1% to 4.7% of their respective 2014 populations.

Alberta and British Columbia had net gains of almost 800,000 people over that same period, with 57% of that total in Alberta.

Young people are of course more responsive to labour market supply-and-demand pressures and are the most frequent participants in interprovincial migration. The Centre for the Study of Living Standards report provides the age profile for interprovincial migrants compared to the general population as shown in figure 3.7.[28]

The most active age category for interprovincial migration in 2014–2015 was 25–35 years. The relatively high proportion of interprovincial migrants under 5 years of age confirms that it is often families with young children who are moving from one province to another. This again has implications for the sustainability of the rural regions and communities that are losing these families.

As indicated above, only 25% of people who move permanently in Canada are interprovincial migrants. The majority who move do so within their home provinces, and in that regard, the dominant trend is

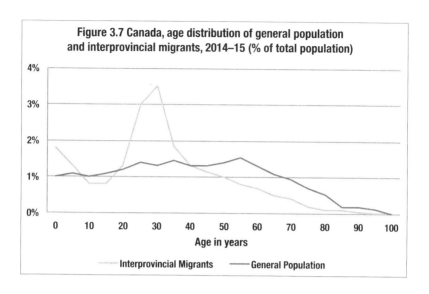

Figure 3.7 Canada, age distribution of general population and interprovincial migrants, 2014–15 (% of total population)

urbanization. Census data confirms that, while the Atlantic provinces remain more rural than the rest of Canada, the forces of urbanization are evident across the region as they still are in Quebec and British Columbia. Figure 3.8 shows changes from the 2001 to the 2016 census in the percentage of population living in "rural and small-town areas" as defined in another recent report by Ray Bollman.[29]

Looking just at Nova Scotia over a recent ten-year period, table 3.6 shows the combined impacts of interprovincial migration and urbanization trends on six rural counties with significant fisheries.[30]

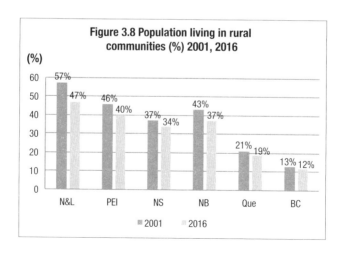

Figure 3.8 Population living in rural communities (%) 2001, 2016

TABLE 3.6 NOVA SCOTIA, CHANGE IN POPULATION SIZE IN COUNTIES WITH SUBSTANTIAL FISHERIES, 2006–2015 (%)			
	2006	2015	% Change
Halifax Regional Municipality	384,548	417,868	+9
Rural counties with economically significant fisheries			
Guysborough	9,220	7,354	-20
Inverness	19,427	17,170	-12
Richmond	9,942	8,956	-10
Shelburne	15,901	14,039	-12
Yarmouth	26,918	24,357	-10
Digby	19,388	17,489	-10

If the same pattern holds true as with interprovincial migration, the majority of people moving from rural to urban areas are prime working-age adults, often with families, leaving disproportionately older rural populations behind.

EVIDENCE OF LABOUR SHORTAGES IN FISHING ENTERPRISES

In a CCPFH telephone survey of Atlantic fish harvesters, conducted in 2015 as part of the FLMI Study, enterprise owners were asked how difficult it had been in the previous two fishing seasons to find crew for their fishing operations. Table 3.7 gives the percentage distribution of responses by province on a five-point scale from *very easy* to *very difficult*. (Prince Edward Island, Manitoba, and British Columbia are not included because of the low survey response rates in those provinces.)

	NL	NS	NB	QC	Atlantic Provinces & Quebec
Very easy	30%	53%	35%	52%	41%
Somewhat Easy	7%	3%	5%	7%	6%
Same	12%	17%	15%	11%	14%
Somewhat difficult	12%	8%	12%	9%	10%
Very difficult	35%	18%	33%	18%	27%

TABLE 3.7 CCCPF 2015 SURVEY RESPONSES BY FISHING ENTERPRISE OWNERS, ATLANTIC PROVINCES AND QUEBEC (%). *How difficult has it been for you over the past two years to find the experienced crew members you need in your fishing operations?*

For all Atlantic and Quebec respondents, 37% reported that it had been somewhat or very difficult to recruit the crew members they needed. Recruitment and retention of crew members appear to be more serious challenges in Newfoundland and Labrador and in New Brunswick, with about 45% of respondents reporting some levels of difficulty in those provinces. Nova Scotia would again appear to be

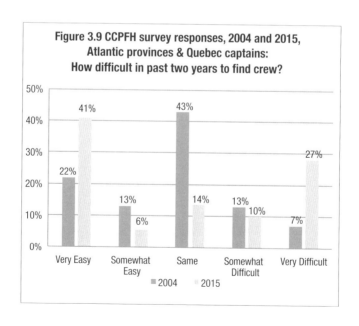

Figure 3.9 CCPFH survey responses, 2004 and 2015, Atlantic provinces & Quebec captains: How difficult in past two years to find crew?

faring better than other provinces, but a quarter of respondents still report some level of difficulty.

The same survey question was used in a CCPFH telephone survey of fish harvesters in 2004. Figure 3.9 combines findings from the 2004 and 2015 surveys in the Atlantic provinces and Quebec to show how crew labour supply conditions may have changed over the period.

This survey evidence suggests a significant shift in the crew labour supply situation for fishing enterprises. In 2004, almost 70% of responses were in the middle area, from somewhat easy to somewhat difficult. In 2015, the responses are more polarized, with only 13% of the captains surveyed reporting no change in level of difficulty, while 43% responded very easy or somewhat easy, and 40% somewhat or very difficult.

In the 2015 CCPFH survey, captains were asked an open-ended question on the reasons why it might be more difficult to find and retain needed crew. The most frequent responses by fishing captains in the Atlantic provinces and Quebec are shown in table 3.8.

TABLE 3.8 CCPFH 2015 SURVEY RESPONSES, FISHING CAPTAINS IN ATLANTIC PROVINCES AND QUEBEC, PERCENTAGE CITING REASONS FOR DIFFICULTIES RECRUITING CREW	
People wanting more weeks of work, or longer seasons, than is typical of fishing employment	84%
People are looking for higher incomes than are typically offered in the fishery	32%
Fewer young people interested in fishing	26%
More crew members reaching retirement age	7%

The more prevalent explanations of labour shortages had to do with capacities to compete in local labour markets on incomes and employment longevity. Many respondents suggested that potential employees are seeking more weeks of work, meaning they are hoping to see a larger portion of their annual income derived from fishing employment. Frequent mention was made in focus groups during the FLMI Study that today's youth are less attracted to a lifestyle of two or three months of work in fishing and a reliance on Employment Insurance (EI) benefits the rest of the year.

INDIGENOUS PEOPLES' PARTICIPATION IN FISHERIES

Given looming labour shortages across most rural coastal regions in Canada, the expanding role of Indigenous peoples in the fishing industry is a positive trend that warrants greater attention. The Canada Census is the best available source of data on Indigenous participation in fishing. (Note that the Canada Census uses the term "Aboriginal" to describe individuals who self-identify as First Nations, Inuit, Métis, or other Indigenous population.) Table 3.9 shows changes from 2001 to 2016 in the numbers of such individuals who identify fishing as a source of employment in provinces with significant commercial fisheries.[31]

TABLE 3.9 CHANGE IN ABORIGINAL PARTICIPATION IN FISHERY, 2001–2016				
	Numbers of Aboriginal individuals employed in fish harvesting		Percentage of Aboriginal individuals in total fish harvester population	
	2001	2016	2001 (%)	2016 (%)
Newfoundland and Labrador	450	690	2	9
Nova Scotia	350	1,370	4	13
Prince Edward Island	60	120	2	4
New Brunswick	410	820	10	18
Quebec	125	370	5	14
Manitoba	495	645	65	77
British Columbia	885	935	22	24

Census data confirms that there were significant increases in the numbers of Indigenous fish harvesters, and Indigenous harvesters grew as a percentage of the total fish harvesting labour force, in all seven of these provinces over the 2001–2016 period. Indigenous harvesters have long had high levels of participation in commercial fisheries in Manitoba and British Columbia.

Given that many Indigenous communities have larger youth populations than non-Indigenous rural communities, there is an important source of new labour supply if barriers to greater participation can be overcome. The challenge, however, is the lack of on-ramps in many regions. In British Columbia, for example, there is a long history of successful Indigenous participation in commercial fisheries, but since the fleet downsizing in the early 1990s, youth in coastal First Nations aren't growing up in the fishery the way they used to and don't have access to the same opportunities to learn by doing.

LESSONS LEARNED

This examination of demographic and labour supply trends in rural regions and their impacts on the fishery leads to a few general conclusions:

- ⊗ Current demographic and labour supply challenges across Canada are being felt more drastically in rural regions and rural industries. Rural working-age populations appear to have been "hollowed out" by the labour mobility trends and industry restructuring programs of the past two decades, with older workers remaining in the labour force while fewer young new entrants came in and many core age (25–45 years) individuals left, often taking their families with them.
- ⊗ For almost all rural coastal regions, none of the three sources of population growth and new labour supply—natural balance, internal migration, and international migration—have seen positive growth.

- Rural-based goods production industries—critically important contributors to national and regional economies—face imminent and critical labour shortages with the potential that a large proportion of the workforce will reach retirement age and exit the workforce over a short period of time.
- The demographic and labour supply challenges taking shape in rural regions and rural industries are already impacting the fish harvesting industry and may intensify more quickly given the nature of fishing work and its generally more remote locations.

The bottom-line finding is that looming demographic and labour supply challenges put the economic growth potential of the fish harvesting industry at risk. Another way of framing the challenge is to recognize that the new labour supply that will be needed as more and more harvesters age out of the industry is not in the industry now, nor is it readily available in most fishing regions of the country. In short, an industry that has been shedding labour for thirty years, based largely in communities that have declining populations over that same period of time, will need to reverse the flow and attract and retain a new labour supply if it is to survive and grow in the future.

Chapter 4

REBUILDING THE FISHERY LABOUR FORCE:

Challenges and Opportunities

To sustain its current economic strength while improving fisheries management and resource stewardship, the Canadian fishing industry will need a stable workforce with requisite knowledge and skills. However, despite dynamic growth in the fishing economy overall the industry now faces a labour supply crisis. There would appear to be three major barriers to overcome: negative perceptions of job opportunities and career prospects in the sector; a history of uncompetitive employment incomes; and increasing difficulty attracting people for seasonal employment.

EMPLOYMENT OPPORTUNITIES
AND CAREER OUTLOOKS

The fishing industry has been shedding jobs since the early 1990s, long enough to shake the family and community foundations from which new labour supply has traditionally been drawn. On the Atlantic coast, the collapse of groundfish stocks in the 1990s displaced some forty thousand fish harvesting and processing workers. With both harvesters and processing workers in the same families in many communities, the local impacts of the shutdown were often serious and long-lasting. In British Columbia the same decade saw radical changes in licensing policies and a 90% fall in the value of wild salmon landings, together resulting in reduced fishing opportunities and fleet downsizing. While the overall Canadian fishing economy began to rebound in the late 1990s with improved prices for seafood products generally, employment in the industry continued to fall off in most fishing regions.

Strange as it may seem, there is no straightforward, definitive way to determine the exact number of people employed in fish harvesting in Canada. DFO keeps track of species licences and vessels but does not directly license or register the harvesters in all provinces, so the department's data system does not provide a definitive picture of who actually fishes.[32]

The Canada Census provides information on the fishing labour force, but with limitations. The mandatory long-form questionnaire asks a sample of respondents what kind of business, industry, or service they work in and what their work or occupation is during the one week in May when the census is conducted. This sampling approach has lower levels of data reliability in rural regions with smaller populations, and it surveys people at only one point in the year. Bearing these data limitations in mind, as shown in figure 4.1, over 16,000 fewer people reported being employed in fishing in 2016 compared to 1991, with 58% of the job loss occurring after 2001, i.e., well after the industry collapses of the early to mid-1990s.

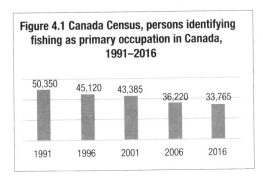

Figure 4.1 Canada Census, persons identifying fishing as primary occupation in Canada, 1991–2016

To access more consistent and rigorous counts, the CCPFH study used Statistics Canada's tax filer database to track changes in the number of individuals actually generating income from fish harvesting employment.[33] While the counts of fish harvesters are significantly higher in the tax filer data, the trends are consistent with the census findings and help explain why a generation of young people growing up in fishing communities has been conditioned to see the fishery as a failing industry with poor employment prospects. With data available up to 2016 at the time of writing, figure 4.2 shows over 13,000 fewer people earning taxable income from fishing jobs—a decline of 24%—over the 2000–2016 period. The decline appears to have bottomed out in 2013, with a 5% recovery by 2016. However, it's not at all clear that the substantial turnaround in the fishery economy since the 2008 global recession has begun to lift employment levels significantly.

Some of the long-term decline in employment resulted from government or industry-led initiatives to reduce the number of fishing vessels to improve economic viability for the remaining enterprises. While often successful in achieving this objective, these initiatives may also have contributed to wider perceptions of shrinking career prospects in the industry.

The scale of job losses varied significantly from province to province. Using tax filer information, figures 4.3 and 4.4

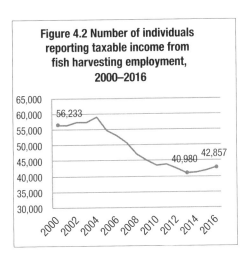

Figure 4.2 Number of individuals reporting taxable income from fish harvesting employment, 2000–2016

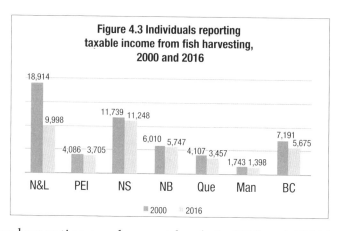

Figure 4.3 Individuals reporting taxable income from fish harvesting, 2000 and 2016

compare harvesting employment levels in 2000 and 2016 in seven provinces with substantial fisheries. Most strikingly, Newfoundland and Labrador saw total fish harvesting employment almost cut in half over the 2000–2016 period. Occurring well after the groundfish moratorium, this decline since 2000 reflects the impacts of fleet restructuring initiatives and accelerating retirements of older harvesters without replacements. Job loss was less dramatic in other Atlantic fisheries, but still significant, particularly in Prince Edward Island and Quebec. Manitoba and British Columbia both saw fishing employment shrink by one-fifth.

The tax filer data distinguishes two categories of income-earning fish harvesters: harvesters who work for regular wages, with employment income reported by T4 slips issued by employers,

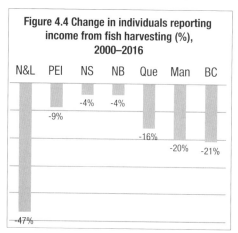

Figure 4.4 Change in individuals reporting income from fish harvesting (%), 2000–2016

and those who are defined as self-employed because they receive incomes based on shares of the value of the catch. For the latter group, employment earnings are reported by T1 slips issued by fish buyers. The self-employed category includes many crew workers as well as many captains who own and operate their own fishing vessels and employ crew. One limitation of tax filer data is that we can't differentiate crew workers from captains when both report as self-employed.

For Canada as a whole, the scale of decline in fishing employment over the 2000–2015 period was similar for both categories, but there were sharp variations among provinces.[34] In Quebec and British Columbia the loss was greatest for self-employed harvesters (figure 4.5). In Newfoundland and Labrador over 80% of waged fishing jobs disappeared while self-employed harvesters were reduced by 37%.

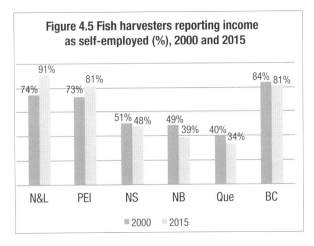

Figure 4.5 Fish harvesters reporting income as self-employed (%), 2000 and 2015

N&L 74% 91%
PEI 73% 81%
NS 51% 48%
NB 49% 39%
Que 40% 34%
BC 84% 81%

■ 2000 ■ 2015

(CCPFH)

Along with these job losses, there also seem to be shifts in how harvesters are remunerated in different fleets and regions. In Newfoundland and Labrador and Prince Edward Island the proportion of harvesters earning self-employment income rose sharply over the 2000–2015 period to become much higher than in the other Maritime provinces and Quebec. In New Brunswick and Quebec the trend seems to be for more harvesters to receive wage income.

There are several possible explanations for these shifts, including changing fleet structures (e.g., fewer large, company-owned offshore vessels) and differences in the length of fishing seasons (e.g., provinces with shorter seasons seem to have more self-employment), but it is also likely that the EI system is an important factor influencing employer and employee decision-making. (More will be said on the role of the EI system in chapter 8.) It is also possible that in fisheries like lobster and snow crab, where gross revenues have risen most significantly, owners may be incorporating their fishing enterprises and now paying wages rather than crew shares to retain more of the incremental earnings in their companies.

(CCPFH)

These overall employment trends are also consistent with changes in the sizes and types of vessels in fishing fleets. The following table (table 4.1), using DFO data, shows shifts in the numbers of fishing vessels in four size classes in the Atlantic and Pacific regions between 2000 and 2017, and also the percentage increase or decrease in each vessel class over the period.[35]

TABLE 4.1 CHANGES IN NUMBERS OF FISHING VESSELS BY LENGTH CLASS, ATLANTIC AND PACIFIC FISHING FLEETS, 2000–2017										
	Vessel Length Classes									
	< 35 ft.		35–45 ft.		45–65 ft.		> 65 ft.		TOTAL	
	#	%	#	%	#	%	#	%	#	%
Newfoundland and Labrador	-3,135	-38	+123	+23	-50	-17	+7	+22	-3,055	-33
Maritimes & Quebec	-1,795	-40	-525	-9	+197	+37	-45	-32	-2,168	-19
British Columbia	-406	-29	-423	-31	-164	-36	-81	-34	-1,074	-31

The information on Newfoundland and Labrador is particularly noteworthy. Over 3,100 vessels under 35 ft.—the type of boat traditionally used in shoreline cod trap and gillnet fisheries—were removed from fishing, contributing to a reduction in the total fleet by one-third. There was, however, a 23% increase in the 35–45 ft. class, the size of vessel most often used in the inshore snow crab, shrimp, and lobster fisheries that have become much more important since the groundfish collapse.

In the Maritimes and Quebec the reduction in small vessels was of a similar proportion to Newfoundland and Labrador (40%), while the core inshore 35–45 ft. class—typical vessels in the lobster fishery—also shrank by over 500 vessels (-9%). In British Columbia the scale of fleet downsizing was relatively consistent across the four vessel classes, in the 29–36% range.

In summary, data from the Canada Census, the Statistics Canada tax filer database, and DFO's vessel licensing registry all help explain why the fishery has not been perceived as a source of stable, long-term employment, and help explain the falling numbers of new entrants to the industry as discussed in the previous chapter.

INCOME TRENDS FOR FISH HARVESTERS

When we think of the fishery, images of chronically low incomes and marginalized communities with shrinking populations come to mind. However, the research evidence paints a more complex, rapidly changing, and in important ways, more positive picture.

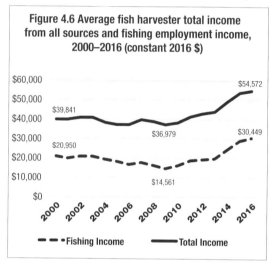

Figure 4.6 Average fish harvester total income from all sources and fishing employment income, 2000–2016 (constant 2016 $)

The economic shocks that hit the industry in the 2000–2016 period—the high Canadian dollar followed by the global recession—did sharply undercut harvester incomes, but the resurgence in the value of fish landings and exports since 2009 has turned things around. Again, using Statistics Canada tax filer data, figure 4.6 shows changes in the average pre-tax income from fishing employment, and total income from all sources, for all Canadians who reported taxable income from fish harvesting jobs over the 2000–2016 period. Bearing in mind that the great majority of fish harvesters experience lengthy periods of the year without employment income from fishing, average earnings from fishing and total incomes would appear to be competitive with other rural industries by 2016.

WAGED AND SELF-EMPLOYED HARVESTERS

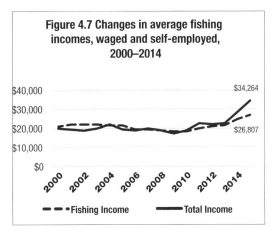

Figure 4.7 Changes in average fishing incomes, waged and self-employed, 2000–2014

Fishing Income   Total Income

As discussed above, there are two categories of fishing workers in terms of employment income: harvesters who receive T4 slips for waged work and self-employed harvesters who are paid shares of the value of the catch.

The surge in the value of fisheries landings and exports has impacted these two categories of fish workers differently. Over the 2000–2015 period for which tax filer information on the two categories was available at time of writing, wage-earning fish harvesters saw a 27% growth in after-inflation fishing income, while self-employed harvesters enjoyed a 73% increase. The two groups began the period at par, but average incomes doubled for harvesters who were paid shares in the value of the catch after 2009 while employment income for wage-earners grew at just half that rate.

PROVINCIAL INCOME TRENDS

There are significant variations in average fishing incomes across the six provinces with the larger-scale commercial fisheries. Figure 4.8 compares average fishing employment incomes in three years: the base year 2000, the bottom of the industry's economic trough in 2009, and the end of the period in 2016. Income figures are in constant dollars indexed to 2016.

Average after-inflation fishing employment incomes increased substantially in five provinces, with most of this growth occurring after 2009. The highest rates of income growth were found in Prince Edward Island and New Brunswick. British Columbia stands out for

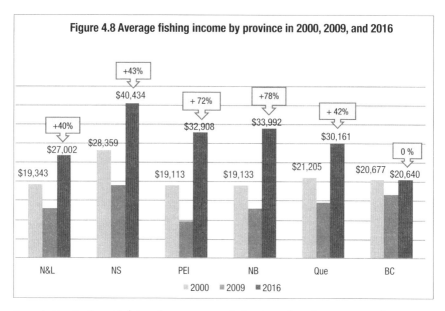

Figure 4.8 Average fishing income by province in 2000, 2009, and 2016

	N&L	NS	PEI	NB	Que	BC
2000	$19,343	$28,359	$19,113	$19,133	$21,205	$20,677
2016	$27,002 (+40%)	$40,434 (+43%)	$32,908 (+72%)	$33,992 (+78%)	$30,161 (+42%)	$20,640 (0%)

its relatively low fishing incomes and the fact that harvesters there saw no growth in after-inflation earnings over the period.

INCOME DISTRIBUTION

One further aspect of fish harvester income trends should be noted. The Gini coefficient is a widely used statistical measure of income inequality. A Gini score of 0 for a given population would represent absolute equality (i.e., every person receiving equal amounts), whereas a score of 1 would mean absolute inequality (i.e., all the income going to one person).

Using tax filer data, the CCPFH study generated Gini coefficients for fishing employment income received by Canadian fish harvesters receiving waged income and self-employment income.

Figure 4.9 shows that over the 2000–2015 period, income inequality measured by the Gini score increased for wage-earning harvesters from 0.57 to 0.59 and for self-employed harvesters from 0.50 to 0.54. Inequality for both groups decreased during the slower years, from 2005 to 2009, then increased sharply as overall income levels recovered from 2010 to 2015.

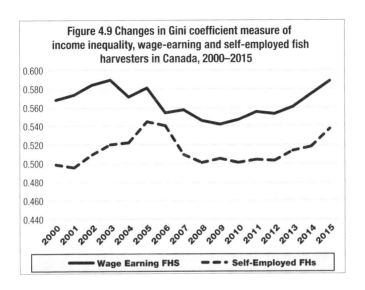

Figure 4.9 Changes in Gini coefficient measure of income inequality, wage-earning and self-employed fish harvesters in Canada, 2000–2015

Wage Earning FHS   Self-Employed FHs

To put these measures in a wider context, the Gini coefficient for the Canadian total population (measured by pre-tax market income) was only 0.44 in 2015, up from 0.43 in 2011.[36] Policy experts often express concern about the potentially negative social and political consequences of increases in income inequality at this level. The evidence suggests that income inequality in fish harvesting is measurably greater than in the wider labour market.

The fact that the self-employed labour force includes many enterprise owner-operators may be part of the explanation, but the trends raise questions about how increasing revenues from surging seafood markets are being distributed across the workforce. In an industry that until recently did not have to compete for labour supply, enterprise owners may soon need to adopt new strategies to recruit and retain the workers they need. And on a longer-term basis, low-paid crew members are unlikely to be positioned financially to take over when retiring owner-operators want to sell their enterprises at fair market value.

THE SEASONALITY CONSTRAINT

In most regions of Canada fishing is of necessity a seasonal industry. In the southern Gulf of St. Lawrence and Quebec, many coastal harbours and bays are blocked by ice for parts of each winter. Fisheries such as salmon, herring, mackerel, and cod are subject to seasonal migrations of fish populations along coastlines or between inshore and offshore waters. And the harvesting of lobster and crab is subject to management plans that protect stocks during spawning seasons.

The CCPFH study generated consistent and convincing evidence that seasonality is a significant barrier to recruitment and retention of new labour supply for fisheries. Fishing employment for between 3 and 7 months leaves large parts of the year with no employment income, particularly in rural communities where other jobs have traditionally been hard to find.

Table 4.2 describes the percentage of the fishing workforce that was employed for different lengths of time, in different provinces, comparing findings from the 2001 and 2016 Canada Census survey questions on weeks worked in the previous year (i.e., 2000 and 2015).

TABLE 4.2 PERCENTAGE OF FISHING WORKFORCE, BY NUMBER OF WEEKS WORKED, BY PROVINCE, 2000 AND 2015

	1–13 weeks		14–26 weeks		27–39 weeks		40–52 weeks	
	2000 (%)	2015 (%)	2000 (%)	2015 (%)	2000 (%)	2015 (%)	2000 (%)	2015 (%)
Newfoundland and Labrador	18	32	61	52	15	9	6	7
Nova Scotia	13	22	39	35	22	18	26	26
Prince Edward Island	18	27	57	46	15	11	10	15
New Brunswick	21	31	58	43	9	10	12	16
Quebec	25	32	62	50	6	7	6	10
Manitoba	29	33	40	37	18	15	13	15
British Columbia	29	26	31	29	13	17	27	29

By these measures there were significant increases over the 2000–2015 period in the proportion of fish harvesters with less than fourteen weeks of fishing employment across the Atlantic provinces and Quebec, suggesting that employment in the industry overall was becoming more seasonal in nature. Nova Scotia had the lowest proportion of harvesters who worked less than fourteen weeks, and—along with British Columbia—higher percentages with twenty-seven weeks or more of employment. But in all provinces except Nova Scotia, 70% or more of harvesters worked in fishing jobs for half the year or less in 2015.

As noted previously, in the 2015 CCPFH survey, 83% of Atlantic respondents identified "people looking for (or leaving for) jobs that are less seasonal" and "people looking for (or leaving for) jobs that offer more weeks of work" as reasons why it was difficult to attract and retain needed crew. As well, about one-third of respondents saw "people looking for (or leaving for) jobs that pay more" as a barrier to finding crew, which is another consequence of limited weeks of employment.

By these measures, trends in the industry have been toward shorter rather than longer periods of employment over the year for many harvesters. In a situation of looming labour supply challenges, it will be necessary to address the seasonality constraint in new and innovative ways if the industry is to attract and retain the new entrants it will need.

BOTTOM LINE

The evidence reviewed here identifies three challenges to rebuilding the fisheries labour force: negative perceptions of an industry that has long been shedding labour, expectations of inadequate employment incomes, and seasonal limitations on employment duration.

The evidence confirms that two of these challenges are real and significant. There has been long-term shrinkage in employment opportunities across the sector, and young people have been conditioned not to look to the industry for attractive career opportunities. As well, seasonally truncated employment has been a fundamental attribute of work in fish harvesting in many fleets and regions, and appears not to be changing. Evidence from community case studies carried out during the CCPFH study confirmed that young people in coastal communities stay in school longer, have more career options, are more mobile in pursuit of jobs, and are much less attracted to seasonal work and repeated reliance on EI during non-fishing seasons.

The good news, however, is that the surge in landed values and seafood export earnings has begun to lift average incomes in most regions and fleets. Many enterprise operators are already in stronger positions to compete for new labour supply by providing incomes attractive enough to draw people from other industries or from other regions. Fish harvesters who are paid in catch shares appear to be benefiting from the improving fishery economy more than those who work for wages.

In an industry with looming labour shortages and a need to compete more effectively to attract and retain new labour supply, new strategies will be needed to change the image of the industry as a career option and to mitigate the limitations on incomes and employment security associated with seasonality. The change will have to begin with enterprise owners facing up to the reality that they need to be more proactive to compete for new labour supply.

Chapter 5

INTERGENERATIONAL SUCCESSION AND THE STRUGGLE OVER ACCESS RIGHTS

Previous chapters have compiled evidence to support three basic assertions about Canada's fishing industry today:

⊗ The overall fishing economy is strengthening on a medium- to long-term trajectory.

⊗ Current demographic and labour supply trends represent the biggest potential limitation on the sustainability of this growth.

⊗ While harvester incomes are improving, and should continue to do so, the capacities of the harvesting sector to compete for new labour supply are limited by the established patterns and related negative perceptions of low incomes and seasonal employment.

If rising global demand continues to drive up the market value of the fish in the water, the rights to harvest that fish—i.e., fishing licences and quotas—will also rise in value and will attract more and more investor interest. If the incomes of new entrant harvesters and crew workers in the industry do not rise in step with the increasing value of what they produce, they will not have the financial resources to purchase fishing enterprises and harvesting rights from the 30–40% of current owner-operators who will age out of the industry over the next decade.

Given rising market demand and product values, we can be certain that someone will harvest the fish, somehow. Current economic and labour supply trends raise a critical policy issue that industry and government leaders will need to address in the coming decade: who will benefit from the unprecedented new wealth being harvested from the sea?

POLICY CHALLENGES

In an October 2017 speech to a meeting with fish harvesters in Nova Scotia, then DFO minister Dominic LeBlanc addressed an emerging concern among harvester organizations. He said,

> Fishing licenses have become over-valued in recent years, especially here in Southwest Nova Scotia. This makes it extremely difficult for young fishermen to access the fishery, and more often than not prevents new entrants altogether. The high upfront cost of a license means that many would-be fishers are excluded from the fishery because they simply do not have access to the large sums of money that fishery licenses have come to cost....
>
> How can we make sure that the benefits of the fishery go to those who work hard to prosecute it, and to the communities that support them? And, harvesters get a fair return for the investments they make in boats and equipment.[37]

POLICY FOUNDATIONS FOR ATLANTIC FISHERIES

Three DFO policies that have been essential to the sustainability of community-based, owner-operator fisheries in Atlantic Canada.

⊗ The Fleet Separation Policy, in place since 1979, prohibits fish processors and other non-harvester interests from owning or controlling fishing licences in most inshore and midshore fleets (i.e., vessels under 65' in length).
⊗ The Owner-Operator Policy (1989) requires licence holders in these fleets to be on-board as captains of the vessels that fish their licences.
⊗ The Preserving the Independence of the Inshore Fleet in Canada's Atlantic Fisheries (PIIFCAF) policy was put in effect in 2007 specifically to eliminate controlling agreements that undermined the Owner-Operator and Fleet Separation Policies.

Harvester leaders have been focusing on this issue for many years. The first national study of human resources trends in the industry, completed by the CCPFH in 2005, identified growing inflationary pressures on licence and quota prices as a threat to owner-operator fleets. It began with an examination of how the market value of a fishing enterprise is determined. "When a willing buyer and seller negotiate the sale of a business and determine a value it is generally considered to be the 'fair market value' defined as the highest price available in an open and unrestricted market between informed and prudent parties, acting at arm's length and under no compulsion to act, expressed in terms of cash. The basic premise is the seller will only sell if the price offered is acceptable and the purchaser believes the negotiated price will provide future economic benefit from the enterprise."[38]

In Atlantic Canada and Quebec, licensing policies—in particular, the Owner-Operator and Fleet Separation policies—restrict ownership of the most valuable licences and fish quota to qualified professional harvesters who own and operate their own fishing enterprises. The objective for these policies is to maintain an "open and unrestricted market" within and exclusive to that defined population of potential purchasers. However, the 2005 CCPFH report identified a changing market environment with two discrete segments: the legitimate owner-operator market and an emerging unrestricted market dominated by "special interest purchasers."

In the owner-operator market the purchase price for a fishing enterprise would normally reflect its fair market value as an independent fish harvesting business with sufficient revenues to sustain harvester owner-operators and their crew members.

In this market environment, the purchase price for a fishing enterprise is a direct reflection of its business value in terms of its capacity to generate revenues, taking account of the risks associated with shifting fish stock abundance and market demand. A harvester with adequate fishing and management skills who purchases the enterprise in this market, using conventional borrowing methods at reasonable interest rates and operating within all the rules, should be able to maintain a viable business (i.e., carry the operating and debt costs and make some level of profit).[39]

In contrast, buyers in the emerging open market segment were less constrained by the immediate challenges involved in sustaining a fish harvesting business. This category included government agencies that, at the time, were purchasing licences and quotas to be transferred to First Nations following the Supreme Court's *Marshall Decision*, and DFO and harvester organizations engaged in fleet reduction or licence buyback programs in certain fisheries. Of most concern, however, was the growing use of "controlling agreements" by processors and fish buyers to secure resource supplies. These were legal workarounds with which non-harvesters were able to purchase the beneficial ownership of licences while keeping the harvester-seller's name on the licence to disguise who actually controlled it. The nominal owner then became an employee of the company with no say in any future disposition of the licence and any attached fish quotas. These transactions directly contravened the Owner-Operator and Fleet Separation Policies, but because they were just policies and not law or regulations, DFO officials in different regions were able to interpret and enforce them with different levels of rigour and "flexibility" in different fleets.

The 2005 CCPFH study confirmed that licence prices were rising significantly in the traditional market segment because special interest purchasers were influencing price expectations among both buyers and sellers. The report drew the following conclusions:

> From the point of view of renewal of the fish harvester labour force, particularly at the level of enterprise heads, the principal challenges associated with rising license values in the traditional owner-operator market are the need to improve access to capital, to build knowledge and skills to manage more valuable businesses, and to innovate in fleet or community-based fisheries management.
>
> The emerging open market, however, raises more complex issues about the relative impacts of different fisheries management models and licensing systems, and ways to regulate markets for privileges to harvest public resources. The major finding of this study with regard to current markets for fisheries access rights is that the open market is expanding rapidly to the point where it threatens to destabilize and indeed to displace the traditional market.[40]

In response to mounting industry pressures, in 2007 Conservative DFO minister Gail Shea put in place a new policy titled Preserving the Independence of the Inshore Fleet in Canada's Atlantic Fisheries (PIIFCAF), to require any fishing licences then held under controlling agreements to be returned to bona fide fish harvester ownership within seven years. PIIFCAF was introduced at a time when the overall fishing economy was in the throes of a downward spiral that would continue through the Great Recession. But the rapid recovery of seafood markets after 2009 has since driven up inflationary pressures on fishing access rights far beyond what was envisioned in the CCPFH analysis of the issue in 2005. As the fish in the water became more and more valuable, conflict over the ownership of harvesting rights intensified. Despite PIIFCAF, different forms of controlling agreements became more evident across the industry, spreading from the lobster fishery in Southwest Nova Scotia to the snow crab and other fisheries in Newfoundland and Labrador and other regions.

"MODERNIZING" THE OWNER-OPERATOR AND FLEET SEPARATION POLICIES

The Canadian fishing industry needs greater ability to respond to changing market conditions and resource fluctuations than that afforded by Canada's current system of fisheries management.... Restrictive licensing rules that do not focus on conservation and vary significantly across the country may serve to impede the economic prosperity of the harvesting sector and discourage investment in the industry. A renewed, nationally consistent approach to fisheries management is needed to create a business environment conducive to economic prosperity in the 21st century. Rules must be re-evaluated for continued need and relevance, management measures must be harmonized, and harvesters must be given the freedom to self-adjust to resource fluctuations and market demands.

FROM DFO MINISTER KEITH ASHFIELD'S 2012 DISCUSSION PAPER ON MODERNIZING CANADA'S FISHERIES ACT

In 2012, a second fisheries minister in the Harper Conservative Government, Keith Ashfield, announced a plan to "modernize" the Fisheries Act, including a thinly disguised intention to eliminate the Owner-Operator and Fleet Separation Policies. The response from the industry was immediate and intense. To fight these changes, harvester organizations across the country came together to form the Canadian Independent Fish Harvesters Federation. A key objective of the CIFHF was to have Owner-Operator and Fleet Separation protections put into legislation so that, unlike mere policies, they could not be cancelled or watered down at the stroke of a minister's pen.

There followed six years of intensive political lobbying for and against the policies, with company-funded court challenges to the minister's authority to enforce PIIFCAF, including appeals to the Supreme Court. With strong support from municipal and provincial governments and many community allies, the CIFHF was successful in stopping the Harper Government from proceeding with major changes to licensing policies. But the struggle did not stop there.

The Fleet Separation Policy was first put in effect in 1979 by then fisheries minister Roméo LeBlanc. In 2018, his son, Liberal DFO Minister Dominic LeBlanc, introduced Bill C-68 to amend the Fisheries Act and, among other things, entrench the Owner-Operator and Fleet Separation Policies in law and regulations.[41] In June 2019, the bill received royal assent, providing future DFO ministers with clear and unequivocal authority and responsibility to give consideration to "social, economic and cultural factors in the management of fisheries" and to "the preservation or promotion of the independence of licence holders in commercial inshore fisheries." New regulations under the act will give Owner-Operator and Fleet Separation protections permanent legal force to specify who can and cannot own fishing licences and quotas.

There are high expectations across the industry that once the new Fisheries Act is fully in force the upward pressure on the market value of fishing rights will be moderated. However, over the medium to long term, the value of licences and quotas will still gravitate to fair market value, reflecting the business revenues that can be generated with them. If the value of seafood products in global markets continues to trend upward—as we expect it to do, barring stock collapses or serious disruptions in international trading relations—licence prices will continue to escalate in value.

Within a more closely regulated industry where ownership of access rights in the most valuable fisheries in Atlantic Canada is restricted to qualified professional harvesters, the new challenge will be to ensure that orderly succession through intergenerational transfers of fishing rights takes place within a rebuilding fish harvester labour force.

INTERGENERATIONAL SUCCESSION

Based on evidence from Statistics Canada's tax filer system and the Canada Census, the CCPFH study anticipated that up to 40% of fishing enterprises in Canada will have changed hands by 2025 as current licence and quota owners age out of the industry. Neither DFO nor any other government agency tracks seller-to-buyer licence transactions, so there is at present no authoritative source of information on trends in the market in fishing licences.

To generate evidence on this issue, the CCPFH labour market study conducted a survey of fish harvesters in 2015 with a number of questionnaire items on matters impacting intergenerational transfers of fishing assets. The survey sample population had acceptable margins of error for three provinces and for fishing captains as a single population across the Atlantic region and Quebec.[42] The age profile of the fishing captains who participated in the survey is shown in table 5.1.[43]

TABLE 5.1 CCPFH 2015 SURVEY, AGE PROFILE OF CAPTAIN-RESPONDENTS, ATLANTIC PROVINCES AND QUEBEC (%)					
	NL	NS	NB	Que	Atlantic
Under 40	4	9	11	18	9
40–54	45	41	43	35	42
55–64	36	32	33	34	34
65 and older	13	16	12	12	14

Respondents were asked to assess the importance of various factors that might influence their decisions to retire and sell their enterprises on a scale of 1 ("Not important at all") to 5 ("Very important"). Figure 5.1 describes the pattern of responses for all Atlantic and Quebec captains.

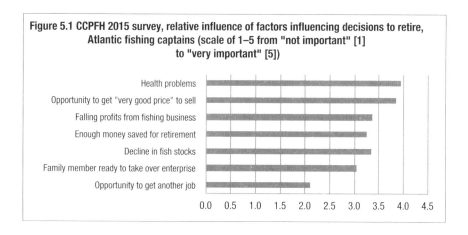

Figure 5.1 CCPFH 2015 survey, relative influence of factors influencing decisions to retire, Atlantic fishing captains (scale of 1–5 from "not important" [1] to "very important" [5])

Responses suggest that "health problems"—a euphemism perhaps for growing older and not being able to manage the physical challenges of fishing work—and the opportunity to get "a very good price" for the enterprise are the most significant factors in decisions to retire. Access to a different job and having a family member ready to take over were seen as least important overall.

Another questionnaire item asked about respondents' objectives when selling or transferring their enterprises at retirement. They were asked: "When you choose to leave the fishery, and sell or transfer your licences, which of the following best describes your goal?"

Figure 5.2 shows the responses from captains in Newfoundland and Labrador and in the Maritime provinces and Quebec together. Keeping the enterprise within the family or community was the highest overall priority in the Maritimes and Quebec, while getting the highest possible price was most strongly emphasized in Newfoundland and Labrador. Anecdotal evidence suggests that the intention to sell to the highest possible bidder may also reflect the growing reality that keeping the licence in the family or community is simply not an option in many areas with declining and aging populations, the more so in Newfoundland and Labrador.

A further survey item inquired about potential buyers in terms of likelihood to pay the "highest price."

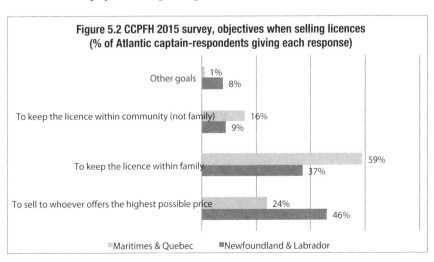

Figure 5.2 CCPFH 2015 survey, objectives when selling licences
(% of Atlantic captain-respondents giving each response)

Other goals — 1% / 8%

To keep the licence within community (not family) — 16% / 9%

To keep the licence within family — 59% / 37%

To sell to whoever offers the highest possible price — 24% / 46%

Maritimes & Quebec   Newfoundland & Labrador

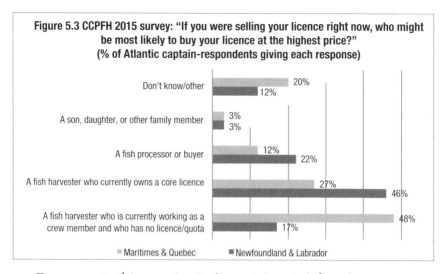

Figure 5.3 CCPFH 2015 survey: "If you were selling your licence right now, who might be most likely to buy your licence at the highest price?" (% of Atlantic captain-respondents giving each response)

- Don't know/other — 20% / 12%
- A son, daughter, or other family member — 3% / 3%
- A fish processor or buyer — 12% / 22%
- A fish harvester who currently owns a core licence — 27% / 46%
- A fish harvester who is currently working as a crew member and who has no licence/quota — 48% / 17%

▪ Maritimes & Quebec   ▪ Newfoundland & Labrador

Responses to this question in figure 5.3 varied sharply across provinces, with captains in Newfoundland and Labrador seeing other core licence holders and fish processors as most likely to pay the "highest price" and working crew members as less likely. This may reflect the wider occurrence in that province of "combining" or "buddying up," where two enterprise owners combine licences to fish together on one vessel. Anecdotal evidence would also suggest that some licence holders in Newfoundland and Labrador and other provinces have used recent profit increases to purchase second licences under the names of family members or crew members to build up multi-licence enterprises.

In Quebec and the Maritimes there are higher expectations of crew members' abilities to meet higher prices. Captains in Newfoundland and Labrador and Nova Scotia more frequently identified fish processors or fish buyers as potential purchasers at the highest prices (22% and 24% respectively). In no provinces were family members seen as likely to be able to pay higher prices, suggesting the potential for tension between the goal to keep enterprises in families and the possibility of windfall capital gains upon retirement.

To generate evidence on possible fishing enterprise buyers, the CCPFH study also surveyed crew workers.[44] With a sample population

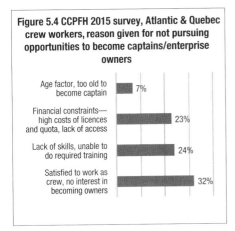

Figure 5.4 CCPFH 2015 survey, Atlantic & Quebec crew workers, reason given for not pursuing opportunities to become captains/enterprise owners

- Age factor, too old to become captain: 7%
- Financial constraints—high costs of licences and quota, lack of access: 23%
- Lack of skills, unable to do required training: 24%
- Satisfied to work as crew, no interest in becoming owners: 32%

of just 372 crew members, 34% of crew respondents in the Maritimes and Quebec but only 19% in Newfoundland and Labrador indicated that they planned to "buy or take over an enterprise and become a captain."

Crew respondents who stated no expectation of becoming enterprise owners were asked the reason for that outlook. The most frequent responses are shown in figure 5.4. Despite a less than robust sample population, the pattern of responses does appear to be consistent with other findings. With an average age of close to 50 across the sample population, a majority of crew respondents would be past the age where they might typically make the transition to becoming owner-operators. That only 25% of crew respondents stated intentions to become enterprise owners would appear to confirm the overarching concern that, even if retiring captains themselves want to keep ownership of their enterprises within their families or communities, there may not be enough harvesters in the ranks now to achieve that outcome.

Survey results from fish harvesters in British Columbia are not included in this consideration because of small sample sizes. However, in this province where Owner-Operator and Fleet Separation Policies are not in effect, and where landed values and harvester incomes have not kept pace with fisheries in eastern Canada, CCPFH community case studies and independent research by Ecotrust Canada confirm that fishing access rights are increasingly out of reach for ordinary fish harvesters who must rely on their fishing incomes to accrue investment capital.[45]

UPWARD PRESSURES ON LICENCE
AND ENTERPRISE PRICES

TABLE 5.2 CCPFH 2015 SURVEY OF ATLANTIC CAPTAINS: "IF YOU WERE TO CHOOSE TO SELL THE TOTAL ENTERPRISE RIGHT NOW WHAT WOULD YOU SUGGEST WOULD BE THE CURRENT MARKET VALUE?"		
	Number of Respondents	Mean Average
Newfoundland and Labrador	138	$238,500
Nova Scotia	146	$518,733
New Brunswick	190	$330,184
Quebec	60	$416,583
Atlantic and Quebec	572	$377,068

A further question on intergenerational transition issues in the 2015 CCPFH survey inquired about estimates of the market value for fishing enterprises, including licences, quotas, vessels, and fishing gear. Table 5.2 shows the average estimates of enterprise selling prices as reported by captains surveyed in the Atlantic region and Quebec.[46] This table provides credible estimates of the market value for most fishing enterprises at the end of the 2015 season. However, fisheries landings and landed values have changed since 2015, with significantly higher landed values and gross revenues in many fleets.

The CCPFH study generated qualitative findings on these issues from focus groups, key informant interviews, and other consultations. For example, in consultations with fish harvester leaders and government officials in the fall of 2017, lobster-based enterprises (including licences, vessels, and gear) were reportedly selling for between $600,000 and $1 million in southeast New Brunswick and Prince Edward Island. These high price levels were described as a reflection of improved landings and prices in many areas during the 2016 and 2017 seasons.

In March 2017, the Maritime Fishermen's Union held a policy symposium attended by some eighty harvester leaders, the majority of them owner-operators in the southern Gulf of St. Lawrence. A poll of attendees identified average prices for lobster licences alone (without vessels and gear) to be in the $300,000–$350,000 range in that region prior to the opening of fishing that year. In the fall of 2017, after a season characterized by improved landings and prices in most areas, some of these same fish harvesters reported that prices for licences alone in their communities had risen above $500,000. In the fall of 2018, after yet another highly productive lobster season, anecdotal evidence suggested that enterprises were selling in the southern Gulf of St. Lawrence for $1 million or more.

On balance and over time, the fair market value for fishing enterprises should go up or down with production levels and market conditions in particular fisheries. The CCPFH survey asked captains to identify the species that provided the most revenue for their fishing businesses. Table 5.3 shows responses across different provinces. Again, responses from Prince Edward Island are not shown separately but are included in the Atlantic total.

TABLE 5.3 CCPFH 2015 SURVEY, RESPONSES OF ATLANTIC CAPTAINS TO: "WHAT THREE SPECIES GENERATED THE MOST REVENUE FOR YOU IN 2015?"

	% of respondents identifying fish species as an important source of fishing revenue				
	NL	NS	NB	Que	Atlantic Total
Snow crab	61%	23%	6%	30%	29%
Lobster	40%	96%	94%	63%	76%
Groundfish (cod, halibut, etc.)	74%	14%	8%	26%	30%
Pelagics (herring, mackerel, capelin, etc.)	15%	17%	28%	12%	20%

These responses suggest that the market value of enterprises will be most heavily influenced by landings and prices for lobster in the Maritimes, whereas snow crab and groundfish are most critical in

(CCPFH)

Newfoundland and Labrador. While lobster is dominant, Quebec fisheries are more evenly distributed across three species. Pelagic species have some importance in all regions as a source of bait for the lobster and crab fisheries and as a supplemental income source, particularly in New Brunswick.

Product values have been increasing across all these fisheries, with shellfish species showing the greatest growth. If these trends continue—and anecdotal evidence confirms that they have done so in 2018 and the spring season of 2019—the fair market value of access rights in most fisheries will almost certainly continue to see upward pressures. In other words, the front-end investment costs for new entrants to become owner-operators will progressively increase in line with the growing value of the fish in the marketplace.

THE POLITICS OF LICENCE MARKETS

Based on the above findings, industry and government planners and policy leaders should assume that issues of accessibility and affordability for new entrants to the fishing labour force will become more pressing and, indeed, controversial with time. In Atlantic fisheries, the evidence suggests that a new entrant harvester wanting to become an owner-operator might have to finance the acquisition of an enterprise worth between $500,000 and $1.5 million, depending on the region and the licences and quota attached to the enterprise. An enterprise with a lobster licence, for example, will be at the high end of that range in Southwest Nova Scotia, in the middle to upper-middle in the southern Gulf of St. Lawrence and Quebec, and at the lower end in Newfoundland and Labrador. Similarly, an inshore enterprise in Newfoundland and Labrador with a sizable snow crab allocation would be at the higher end of the scale. The critical challenge will be to ensure that new entrant harvesters who begin their fishing careers as apprentice crew workers will be able to advance over a reasonable time period to become owner-operators of enterprises they purchase at such cost levels.

This discussion assumes that the transaction occurs within the traditional owner-operator market where the enterprise would be the new owner's primary or sole source of business income and debt obligations would be met out of fishing revenues. However, despite the new Fisheries Act, other actors may continue to exert upward pressures on the value of licence and fish quota prices.

Fishing captains who are more successful than others in competitive fisheries like lobster are finding ways to purchase second enterprises as investments, putting them in the name of a family member or dependent crew member. Such "high liner" fishing captains can often make purchases with little or no debt financing, and therefore may pay higher front-end prices.

Under DFO licensing rules in some fleets—most commonly in Newfoundland and Labrador—one owner-operator can buy a second enterprise to combine with one already owned and reduce operating costs significantly by using just one vessel and one crew, possibly selling off the redundant vessel and gear to help finance the purchase. In these cases, the seller joins the crew of the combined enterprise as a nominal partner. Again, such purchasers are able to pay higher prices for licences, thus bidding up their value.

Fish buyers and processors are still taking control of enterprises through under-the-table agreements to secure raw material supplies, having dependent fish harvesters serve as nominal owners and vessel operators.

Fish buyers and processors also lend money to fish harvesters to purchase enterprises in return for exclusive access to the catch at prices controlled by the buyer/processor.

Government agencies provide funds to First Nations to purchase fishing enterprises or make direct purchases to transfer assets to Indigenous communities.

Investors from outside the industry have purchased fishing enterprises, again with fish harvesters as nominal owners, purely as a speculative investment in anticipation of significant growth in the profitability of the enterprise or in the market value of the asset.

Any one of these non-traditional buyers is positioned to purchase fishing enterprises at price levels higher than fair market value within a traditional owner-operator market. And we must assume that if global market demand for seafood continues to build up, more non-traditional investors will want to profit from this growth by acquiring ownership or control of fishing access rights.

In British Columbia, where fleets operate without Owner-Operator and Fleet Separation protections, non-harvester investors are highly active in the market for licences and quotas, including recently identified cases of illegal money laundering. Most traditional owner-operators wanting to acquire more fishing rights in British Columbia cannot compete with the prices paid by these types of buyers, and so have to lease quota or licences at cost levels that limit enterprise viability. This may help to explain the research evidence that relatively few crew members in British Columbia anticipate becoming enterprise owners.

One complicating factor is the role fish buyers and processing companies have traditionally played in helping harvesters finance their operations. Harvesters have always borrowed from their local fish buyers in return for commitments to deliver raw material to the lenders' plants. Many young harvesters have received loans from their local processor to become owner-operators and, generally speaking, harvester organizations don't object to such transactions as long as they do not involve controlling agreements. But with licence prices rising to current levels, fish processors are demanding greater security for such lending and stronger guarantees that the harvesters they finance will deliver fish to them at price levels they control.

In Nova Scotia, for example, the Western Nova Scotia Lobster Dealers Coalition was recently formed to lobby on this issue. Robert Thibault, a former DFO minister and spokesperson for the coalition, defended the use of controlling agreements as a necessary hedge against defaults on high-value loans. The coalition submitted a proposal asking the federal government to grant processors the authority to give loans to harvesters with the same forms of security as a bank. Thibault explained the proposal as follows in a CBC interview:

> [Processor companies] could put out the money, they would hold the mortgage and then they would have a business arrangement with a person owning the licence where they would, I assume, buy the product....If the owner or captain wanted to get out of the arrangement, they would pay off the debt and move on as they do with the banks....I think it's important that we find a legal way, an above-board way for the buyers and the fishermen to get into a contractual agreement.[47]

Hubert Saulnier, a prominent harvester leader in Southwest Nova Scotia is somewhat unusual in that he actively defends owner-operator fisheries but sold his enterprise to a company and now fishes under a controlling agreement. In a CBC interview he defended such agreements: "This has been going on for 30 years....As a matter of fact, it's got a lot of entrants into [Lobster Fishing Area] 34, and right now they are doing quite well. These young guys—not old like me—started working, running a boat for a company lobster fishing, working hard, day and night. They made some money, put the money aside—then they quit the company and bought their own rigs....Twenty per cent of the boats in Meteghan wouldn't have got started in the industry without some help."[48]

Fish harvester organizations that oppose controlling agreements identify two serious flaws in the arguments put forward by Thibault and Saulnier. First, the participation of more and more non-harvester buyers in the market for licences and quota progressively inflates prices beyond fair market value for regular working harvesters, putting greater pressure on enterprise viability for new entrant harvesters who have to buy in at higher prices and incur higher debt levels. There is potential for negative outcomes in terms of more intensive pressures on fish stocks and increased accidents at sea as new owner-operators fish more aggressively to stay afloat under heavy debt burdens.

Second, if buyers and processors consolidate control over more licences, they will have more leverage to control fish prices and transfer profit shares from primary producers to higher levels in the value chain. This in turn will reduce the business viability of enterprises, making it even more difficult for new entrants to become owner-operators, and taking more wealth out of fishing communities.

As shall be seen in chapter 9, these are exactly the outcomes being identified in British Columbia where there is an open market for licences and quota.

MANAGING THE LICENCE MARKET

This chapter began by quoting Minister LeBlanc's statement that "fishing licenses have become over-valued in recent years." The core issue that emerges is there are various ways to measure the value of fishing enterprises and to determine if they are over-valued. The evidence confirms new baseline realities.

First, a large portion of Canadian fishing enterprises will change hands within the next decade as up to 40% of current owner-operators age out of the industry. Due to financial constraints and demographic and labour mobility trends, there are insufficient numbers of crew workers currently in the industry, or potential new entrants in fishing communities, who are well positioned to take over these enterprises.

Second, barring a cataclysmic collapse in fish landings or global seafood markets, the fair market value of fishing enterprises will progressively increase in response to improving fish prices, expanding profitability and confidence in future business growth.

Notwithstanding the new Fisheries Act, higher profitability levels will continue to attract interest from non-traditional investors inside and outside the industry and will amplify processor efforts to secure resource supplies.

It is a matter of growing concern for harvester leaders that the increasing market value of fishing enterprises holds potential to sow divisions among harvesters and their organizations, pitting the interests of sellers against those of aspiring new entrant buyers. If an oversupply of enterprises for sale takes shape relative to the number of available traditional purchasers, and this oversupply causes a fall in licence prices below reasonable estimates of enterprise value based on profitability, there could be growing pressure on DFO ministers for greater "flexibility" to increase the pool of potential buyers.

These possibilities speak to a wider policy challenge that reaches beyond the fishing industry: how do government and the wider society manage and protect vital socio-economic assets that have different values in different markets? The most familiar example is fertile agricultural land in regions like the Niagara Peninsula in Ontario and the Fraser River Delta in British Columbia. In such settings, retiring farmers can sell their land to other farmers for one price or to housing or commercial property developers for a much higher value. A young person wanting to farm that land can finance the purchase at the lower price but would have a failing business if they had to buy it at the market value associated with residential or commercial land development.

Similar issues arise in big-city housing markets when local or foreign interests purchase properties as speculative investments. The resulting inflation in prices distorts decision-making by other buyers and sellers, and disadvantages lower income renters and purchasers. In these situations, all three levels of government have responded to the need for legislative and regulatory mechanisms to protect broadly defined public interests in the long run.

Hopefully, the new Fisheries Act and its attendant regulations will mitigate current distortions in markets for fishing rights in Atlantic

Canada and open up progressive new policy options in British Columbia, but the evidence generated by the CCPFH study would suggest that more extensive efforts will be needed if the policy objectives pursued by both Roméo and Dominic LeBlanc are to be achieved in the medium to long term. These alternative approaches will be further explored in chapter 10.

Chapter 6

MEETING THE SEASONALITY CHALLENGE

As *identified in chapter 4, one of the most serious barriers to attracting* new entrants to the fishery is the seasonal nature of the work. This is a complex issue with a long history. For decades, the structure of the fishing industry was shaped by an oversupply of labour. With chronically high unemployment in rural coastal regions, there were always people needing to take up the available seasonal jobs. Many economists have blamed an overreliance on abundant low-cost labour for long-standing issues of industry overcapacity, low productivity, and lack of innovation, most detrimentally in the processing sector. However, for rural workers with limited schooling and jobs training, a few months of work on a fish boat or in a processing plant provided an income base and "stamps" to qualify for Unemployment Insurance (UI) benefits or (after 1996) Employment Insurance (EI) benefits through the winter months. With low housing costs and little debt, a family with two adults working in low-paid seasonal jobs could get by.

But the days of labour oversupply in coastal regions are coming to an end. A large proportion of the rural seasonal workforce in tourism, food processing, farming, and fisheries is now at retirement age, and we already see widespread reliance on temporary foreign workers in these sectors to keep plants and businesses going. Young people entering the labour force in rural regions generally have higher levels of schooling and post-secondary education and are more mobile than in the past, used to looking for more attractive job opportunities in nearby urban centres or other provinces. The western oil boom in the early 2000s drew thousands of young people away from rural communities on both coasts, and many may never return.

But one strategy people in rural communities continue to use to manage the limitations of seasonal industries is to work in different sectors and occupations over the course of the year. The CCPFH FLMI study assessed the extent to which this tradition of *occupational pluralism* (OP) persists in current labour markets and examined the role it now plays, and potentially could play in future, in sustaining the fisheries labour force.

THE CONTINUING REALITY OF OCCUPATIONAL PLURALISM

Historically, Canadian fisheries evolved within a rural semi-subsistence economy in which OP was an essential element. Prior to the Second World War, many rural families sustained themselves by combining fishing and farming activities with hunting and trapping, lumbering, craft production, and perhaps some wage-paying jobs at home or away. For example, thousands of rural Maritimers took the "harvest trains" every fall to work in the Prairie grain harvest or travelled to the "Boston States" for labouring jobs in winter.

This way of life faded following the Second World War, with the mechanization of agriculture and forestry work, urbanization, and expanding wage employment. Nevertheless, seasonal industries—agriculture, fisheries, forestry, and tourism—remained the mainstays of provincial economies in Atlantic Canada and for many rural regions in other provinces. Working in these sectors became synonymous with social and economic marginality, and out-migration from rural regions continued through the 1940s and 1950s.

The introduction of Unemployment Insurance (UI) in the late 1940s, and its expansion in the 1950s, lifted rural seasonal workers out of severe poverty and made it possible for seasonal industries to retain labour supply. Since then, working in other jobs outside fishing seasons has been a choice rather than an absolute necessity for most fish harvesters and other seasonal workers across Canada.

In its current forms, OP often occurs within families when one spouse works in the service sector while the other runs a farm or fishing operation. We also see fish harvesters operating their own enterprises for short fishing seasons and then crewing on someone else's vessel in a different region or fleet. In recent years, we've heard anecdotal evidence of captains and crew from the southern Gulf of St. Lawrence and Newfoundland and Labrador working as crew during the winter lobster fishery in the Bay of Fundy and Southwest Nova Scotia. Such employment mobility, within and outside the fishery, has long been key for crew workers wanting to build up capital to become owner-operators.

The CCPFH labour market study addressed strategic questions about OP: How much is it happening today, and what are its modern forms? Who participates in it, and why? What kinds of jobs best suit fish harvesters outside fishing, and why? And most importantly, could OP be encouraged, regulated, and facilitated to help mitigate labour supply challenges? Through the research and consultations, a further question emerged that is also critical to this discussion: Would an expansion of OP undermine long-term efforts to professionalize the fish harvesting labour force by encouraging more part-time or occasional attachment to the industry?

OCCURRENCE OF OP IN
THE FISHERIES LABOUR FORCE

The Statistics Canada tax filer system provides data on sources of income and locations where income was earned. With this information we can identify the numbers and characteristics of fish harvesters who reported taxable income from non-fishing jobs along with earnings from fishing.

The tax filer data confirms that OP remains an important income source for fish harvesters in Canada and is particularly significant during periods when fishing income is reduced for various reasons. Figure 6.1 shows the percentage of fish harvesters in Canada who earned taxable income in non-fishing jobs over the 2000–2016 period. This evidence confirms that participation in OP employment ramped up during the economic downturn from 2001 to 2009, but then tailed off as the fishing economy rebounded after 2009.

There is one important qualification on this interpretation: through this period the average age of fish harvesters increased from 41 to 47, and—as we shall see below—OP employment is more common among younger individuals. The steady fall-off in OP engagement after 2010 may also reflect the changing age profile of the harvester workforce as well as improved income from fishing.

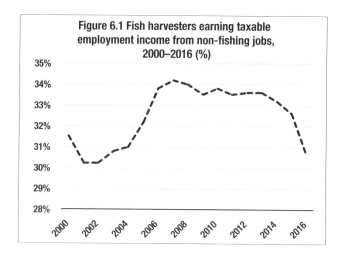

Figure 6.1 Fish harvesters earning taxable employment income from non-fishing jobs, 2000–2016 (%)

OP employment patterns vary across regions and fisheries. Again, using tax filer data, figure 6.2 shows that in four of seven provinces with significant commercial fisheries, harvesters' participation in OP decreased over the 2000–2016 period, and only Newfoundland and Labrador saw a marked increase, while Prince Edward Island stood out for its higher level of OP participation.

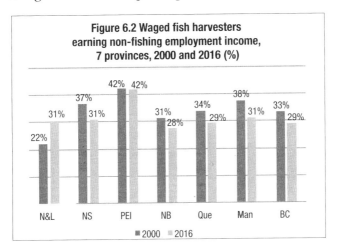

Figure 6.2 Waged fish harvesters earning non-fishing employment income, 7 provinces, 2000 and 2016 (%)

The most important takeaways here are that a consistent 30% of Canadian fish harvesters engages in OP with variations across regions and fleets, and that OP plays an important role in sustaining harvesters in a seasonal industry that is vulnerable to economic ups and downs.

OP INCOMES

Figure 6.3 provides information on changes in average pre-tax incomes for fish harvesters from fishing and non-fishing employment in Canada over the 2000–2016 period, all in constant dollars (2016).[49] The averages for non-fishing employment are given only for those harvesters who received that source of income. The dotted lines in the chart are linear progression lines. i.e., statistical representations of the long-term trends behind the short-term ups and downs.

Three important points emerge from this information. First, average non-fishing employment income did grow substantially in

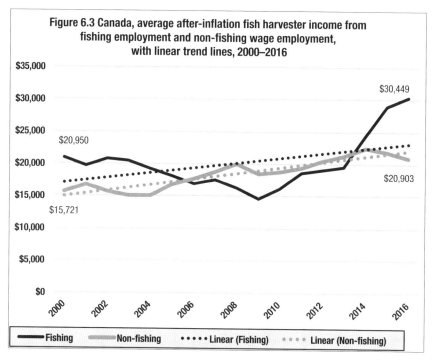

Figure 6.3 Canada, average after-inflation fish harvester income from fishing employment and non-fishing wage employment, with linear trend lines, 2000–2016

after-inflation value, ending the period at almost $21,000. During the recession years, from 2006 to 2013, it actually exceeded average fishing incomes for harvesters in Canada. Harvesters who engaged in OP saw a one-third improvement in after-inflation income from this source over the 2000–2016 period, with the rate of growth levelling off after 2008.

Second, fishing income remains the more important source of income outside the down years, having increased by 45% in after-inflation value over the 2000–2016 period, and by a remarkable 109% from 2009 to 2016. The chart visually confirms the inverse relationship between fishing and OP earnings: when one goes up, the other falls off.

And third, the linear trend lines (i.e., statistical representations of longer-term trends) suggest that both fishing and non-fishing employment income are on track for long-term and significant growth, barring major economic disruptions.

Figure 6.4 shows the changes in non-fishing employment income

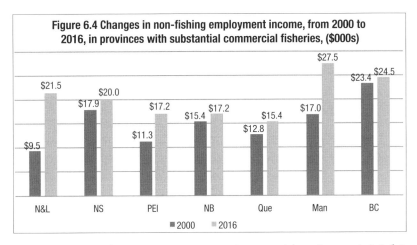

Figure 6.4 Changes in non-fishing employment income, from 2000 to 2016, in provinces with substantial commercial fisheries, ($000s)

between 2000 and 2016 in seven provinces with substantial fishing industries.

Non-fishing employment income was highest at the end of the period in Manitoba and British Columbia. The level of participation in OP employment was not markedly different in these two provinces, so this might indicate that those harvesters who work outside fishing do so with greater intensity, due perhaps to short seasons or more limited fishing opportunities. In Manitoba, for example, one of the most important fisheries involves fishing through the lake ice in deep winter, so some harvesters who engage in this fishery might have the spring, summer, and fall periods available to pursue other jobs.

Another notable feature in figure 6.4 is the sharp increase in average OP income (+126%) earned by harvesters in Newfoundland and Labrador, jumping from the lowest to the highest earners among Atlantic provinces and Quebec over the period.

MOTIVATIONS FOR OP

The 2015 CCPFH survey of fish harvesters asked captain and crew respondents in the Atlantic provinces and Quebec about their experiences with and views on employment outside the fishery. Table 6.1 summarizes responses from 788 captains and 372 crew workers on items pertinent to OP.

TABLE 6.1 CCPFH 2015 SURVEY, SUMMARY OF RESPONSES ON OP ITEMS, ATLANTIC CAPTAINS AND CREW (N=NUMBER OF RESPONDENTS)

	Atlantic captains N=788	Atlantic crew N=372
Per cent having non-fishing jobs in previous 12 months	22%	22%
Location of the non-fishing job (% of those who had non-fishing jobs)		
In the local area	63%	67%
Outside local area, but within the province	20%	24%
Out of province	17%	9%
Years employed in this non-fishing job (median score)	10 years	7 years
Days employed in this job in in previous 12 months (median score)	104 days	92 days
Earnings from this job in previous 12 months (median score)	$20,000	$10,500
Main reasons given for having additional job outside fishing for those who did have such jobs (% of responses)		
To supplement fishing income, for income security, to save money	46%	77%
Due to seasonal nature of fishery; a need to diversify income sources	23%	10%
To keep busy, avoid boredom, maintain job skills	24%	15%
Due to bad year in fishery; needed additional source of income	18%	No mention
To develop or maintain status in another trade or occupation	No mention	15%
Main reasons given for not having an additional job outside fishing for those who did not have such jobs (% of responses)		
No local jobs available; could not find jobs	41%	46%
Long fishing season; no time to work elsewhere	39%	30%
Earned an adequate income in fishery	17%	17%
Age factor—"too old to work away"	5%	4%
Lack of qualifications to access other jobs	5%	6%

About three-fifths of captains and crew who worked outside the fishery did so in their local areas. Interestingly, captains were more likely to travel outside their home provinces than crew members. Respondents appeared to stick with the same non-fishing jobs for lengthy periods—on average, 10 years for captains and 7 for crew. Work periods in non-fishing jobs appear to be for 18 to 20 work weeks.

The dominant objective for OP employment was clearly income supplementation, and more so for crew members. Maintaining diverse job skills, trade status, or links to alternative careers are also significant goals for taking jobs outside fishing.

The pattern of responses by respondents who don't participate in OP seems to indicate that close to half the non-participants felt they had adequate incomes and sufficient work over the year from fishing jobs, while half suggested they would more likely take up other employment opportunities if the jobs were available locally, or if they acquired the qualifications to do other jobs.

The 2015 CCPFH survey of Atlantic region and Quebec crew members (sample size 372) asked additional questions about OP in fisheries-related sectors.

TABLE 6.2 CCPFH 2015 SURVEY, EMPLOYMENT EXPERIENCE: CREW MEMBERS IN ATLANTIC REGION AND QUEBEC (N=372)	
Average years working as crew	17 (median score)
# skippers worked for during fishing career	2 (median score)
Per cent having non-fishing jobs in previous 12 months	22%
Worked in the shoreline or onshore marine harvest (e.g., harvesting clams, oysters, mussels, seaweed, etc.) for at least part of the previous 12 months	14%
Worked in a seafood processing or fish plant job for at least part of previous 12 months	8%

With 22% of crew workers reporting non-fishing employment, the additional survey findings shown in table 6.2 suggest that over 40% of crew workers generated employment earnings outside their primary jobs on fishing vessels.

WHO PARTICIPATES IN OP?

The tax filer data provides useful information on the age-related aspects of OP. Figure 6.5 shows the percentage of fish harvesters in each age group who earned employment income in non-fishing waged jobs in 2016. Over half of fish harvesters in Canada under 25 years old, and two-fifths of those 25–34, were active in OP.

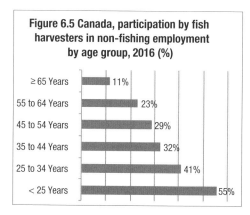

Figure 6.5 Canada, participation by fish harvesters in non-fishing employment by age group, 2016 (%)

Figure 6.6 adds to this picture, showing the age profiles in 2016 of harvesters who earned income in non-fishing jobs and those who did not. Of the harvesters who earned non-fishing employment income, 55% were under the age of 45, compared to 35% of those who did not participate in OP.

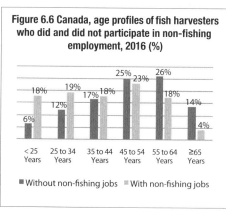

Figure 6.6 Canada, age profiles of fish harvesters who did and did not participate in non-fishing employment, 2016 (%)

This evidence provides strong confirmation that OP activity decreases with age across the labour force, or—expressed differently—younger harvesters are much more occupationally mobile than their older colleagues. This makes sense in different ways: enterprise owners are generally older than their crew workers and earn higher incomes, so perhaps feel less pressure to work in the off-season. Lower-paid crew workers, on the other hand would be more likely to seek additional income sources and some would want to generate savings to become owner-operators. They might also have young families and more financial needs relative to their older counterparts.

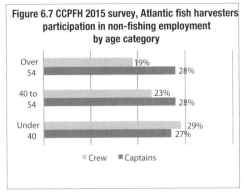

Figure 6.7 CCPFH 2015 survey, Atlantic fish harvesters participation in non-fishing employment by age category

With the 2015 CCPFH survey, cross-tabulations by age and educational level add further nuance to this issue. For fishing captains in the Atlantic provinces and Quebec, the survey responses indicate that among captains, participation in non-fishing employment is consistent across all the age groups at around 28%, while it declines for crew workers with age.

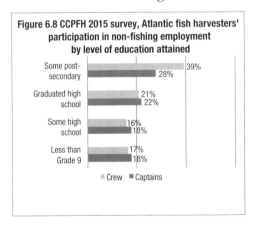

Figure 6.8 CCPFH 2015 survey, Atlantic fish harvesters' participation in non-fishing employment by level of education attained

The survey also asked respondents to identify their highest level of formal education attained. When cross-tabulated with participation in non-fishing employment, the results suggest that participation in non-fishing employment is positively correlated with level of education attained, more emphatically so for crew workers. Nearly 40% of crew with some post-secondary education or training reported being active in OP.

This tax filer and survey evidence taken together supports the overall conclusion that greater participation in OP is associated with being younger and having higher levels of formal education.

OPINIONS ABOUT OP

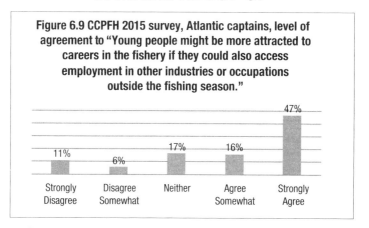

Figure 6.9 CCPFH 2015 survey, Atlantic captains, level of agreement to "Young people might be more attracted to careers in the fishery if they could also access employment in other industries or occupations outside the fishing season."

The 2015 CCPFH survey also included questionnaire items about attitudes toward OP as a means to attract and retain new labour supply. The first question (figure 6.9), addressed to fishing captains in the Atlantic region and Quebec, asked how much respondents agreed or disagreed on a five-point scale with the statement that "Young people might be more attracted to careers in the fishery if they could also access employment in other industries or occupations outside the fishing season." The pattern of responses suggests an openness to the use of occupational pluralist strategies to attract and retain new labour supply; nearly two-thirds of responding captains somewhat or strongly agreed with the statement.

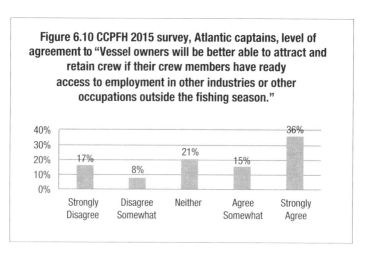

Figure 6.10 CCPFH 2015 survey, Atlantic captains, level of agreement to "Vessel owners will be better able to attract and retain crew if their crew members have ready access to employment in other industries or other occupations outside the fishing season."

A second question (figure 6.10) asked captains whether an OP approach might help enterprise operators attract and retain crew workers. Support for OP on this item is less emphatic than for the previous question, with just over half the respondents agreeing somewhat or strongly, and 25% disagreeing to some extent. Nevertheless, this and the previous item suggest that fishing captains and enterprise heads do see encouragement of OP as potentially helpful for addressing labour recruitment and retention challenges.

EVIDENCE ON OP FROM STAKEHOLDER CONSULTATIONS

In addition to tax filer and survey data, the community case studies carried out as part of the CCPFH study generated qualitative findings on OP issues. This research and consultation work included focus groups and key informant interviews with industry representatives, community leaders, local government officials, and human resources development agencies.[50]

The community studies found pronounced variations in the patterns of OP participation in different regions. In every area key informants described well-established local patterns of harvesters working outside fishing seasons in jobs such as carpentry and construction over their careers. Inter-regional and interprovincial migration for work was seen to be more prevalent in a few areas such as southeast New Brunswick and the Bonavista region of Newfoundland and Labrador. Proximity to urban centres was also a factor. Focus group participants and other key informants generally agreed that crew members tended to engage in OP more than skippers. Informants in different areas identified forms of OP within fisheries (working on multiple enterprises), in other marine sectors (aquaculture, boatbuilding), and outside marine sectors (forestry, harvesting and processing jobs in agriculture, oil and gas exploration and production, carpentry) that reflected the available opportunities in locally accessible labour markets.

The community studies also exposed some ambivalence among fishing captains about the risks of promoting OP as a strategy to address labour market issues. There were concerns that training in other industries and trades could encourage crew to leave the fishery for better employment options elsewhere, and that this would contribute to crew shortages and higher labour costs. Some focus group participants also worried that pursuit of expanded OP might be part of a wider government effort to eliminate or reduce fish harvesters' access to EI.

Harvester leaders in some provinces raised serious concerns about possible unintended consequences of promoting OP. In Newfoundland and Labrador leaders are grappling with the issue of fish harvesters who also maintain good-paying careers in offshore energy, the marine transportation sector, or the oil and gas sector in Alberta. According to tax filer data, in 2013 nearly three hundred individuals who earned taxable income from fishing employment in the province also reported taxable earnings in Alberta. Growing numbers of such individuals have been pressing for flexibility in harvester certification standards to be able to come back to the province to fish for short periods during the most productive seasons. This is seen as taking fishing opportunities and quota away from people who work in the fishery year-round, relying on it as a primary source of income.

The professionalization regimes in Newfoundland and Labrador and in Quebec and DFO's current Independent Core licensing regime were established to help eliminate "moonlighters" and other occasional participants who enter the fishery only during the most lucrative periods, but for whom fishing is not a primary occupational commitment. If not well thought-out and carefully managed, expansion of OP could result in greater flexibility to provide such people greater access, thus draining fishing opportunities and revenue sources away from committed professionals.

With the accelerating return of cod stocks, the industry in Newfoundland and Labrador is currently planning on a transition from specialized seasonal fleets, concentrated largely on shellfish (snow crab and shrimp), to multi-licence enterprises that will harvest a diverse range of shellfish, groundfish, and pelagic species over the year. Industry leaders see a future in which many, if not most, fishing enterprises will be 8–10-month operations and much better positioned to compete for new labour supply with higher wages or crew shares. Though this industry development strategy is still in its early stages, harvester leaders have concerns that OP will be advocated by groups wanting to maintain the status quo of specialized fleets and highly seasonal operations.

In meetings with industry stakeholders in Quebec, concerns were raised about undermining professionalization and also about the

(iStock)

danger that training harvesters to work in other sectors could actually encourage needed workers to exit the industry. Concerns were expressed as well about changes to EI rules that would force harvesters to take up jobs away from their homes and families, which can be especially stressful for people living in more isolated communities. In high unemployment regions, some key informants had concerns that expanded OP might mean that fish harvesters who already earn incomes and qualify for EI would be competing for jobs in fish processing and other sectors during non-fishing seasons and thereby take jobs, incomes, and access to EI away from other community members.

Industry stakeholders in Manitoba were in agreement that OP is a valid approach to making a living in the fishery but observed that job opportunities are limited in many fishing communities, particularly in the north. The most common option for income supplementation was to work for local governments. Opportunities outside the community were seen to require significant relocation costs and living away from home would interfere with pre- and post-season fisheries-related work. There are additional and unique challenges for Indigenous harvesters to live and work away from their communities.

In the case studies in British Columbia many stakeholders held the view that OP can only work as a way to help rebuild labour supply if the fishery itself is stabilized and better managed. New entrant harvesters will need to know that they have secure employment and good career prospects in the sector before they can begin to develop OP options for more clearly defined non-fishing seasons. It was felt that it will be difficult to find non-fishing jobs in more isolated communities and that the focus should be on marine work. However, employers are more often looking for full-time employees, and their high and low demand periods don't correspond with fishing seasons. There was broad consensus that people have always used OP as a survival strategy but to expand it will require greater access to job opportunities and better co-operation from employers. In many of these discussions, OP was described as harder to pursue today than in the past.

In all the community case studies, there was evidence of a sharp and quite interesting disjuncture between the fish harvesters' perception of local labour markets and the views of local community and business leaders outside the fishery. Fish harvesters more often described a lack of available employment opportunities outside the fishery and expressed concern about the negative consequences of greater competition for those jobs, while non-fishing observers agreed strongly that their local economies were more challenged by looming labour shortages than by oversupply. Observers with the latter perspective seemed open to expanding OP as a way to address overall labour market challenges through the more efficient use of available supply across the seasons, while fish harvesters were more likely to downplay such options. All this suggests that the availability of up-to-date information on the trends in local labour markets is a critical factor in shaping attitudes toward OP.

TAKEAWAYS ON OP

The evidence reviewed above indicates that OP plays an important, if not essential, role in sustaining a committed labour force for the fish harvesting industry. Close to one-third of fish harvesters in Canada were employed outside their primary fishing jobs where they earned average incomes of $21,000 in 2016. The 2000–2016 period saw a major downturn in the fishing economy during the Great Recession, and OP jobs, along with EI, provided stability and income security for many harvesters who might not otherwise have remained in the industry.

The available data suggests that over the 2000–2016 period, the percentage of fish harvesters who took up non-fishing employment remained stable overall but did increase sharply during the recession. While OP incomes as a proportion of total incomes did not change markedly over the period, there was continuous growth in after-inflation earnings.

A critically important finding is that, while the overall fishing labour force is aging rapidly and significant numbers of younger people have left the industry over the past two decades, the younger cohorts have markedly higher rates of participation in OP employment than older harvesters. As a supplementary income source, a way to generate savings to become owner-operators, and an alternative to dependence on EI benefits year after year, OP is clearly an important option for younger people now in the industry and a potentially attractive option for those who might consider coming in.

The findings from the harvester survey and the community case studies confirm that OP is a long-established part of how people make a living in the fishery in most regions, and there is cautious receptivity to exploring ways to develop and promote it more effectively to meet future labour supply challenges. Many industry stakeholders seem open to considering the expansion of OP to attract and retain new labour supply, but they are not certain it will be possible to overcome the lack of off-season employment opportunities in rural regions.

Stakeholders do identify risks and possible unintended consequences that would need to be managed in any effort to develop new and expanded forms of OP. The most serious concerns are that more crew workers might leave the industry through training and access to more rewarding jobs, that access to EI might be curtailed, and that professionalization regimes could be undermined if there is greater flexibility in licensing and registration rules to allow more part-time and marginally attached people into the industry.

There is also the possibility that putting greater priority on OP might distract attention away from opportunities to restructure fleets and fishing plans to lengthen seasons, diversify fishing operations and improve enterprise viability, thereby improving industry capacities to compete more successfully for new labour supply.

Given these complex factors, the critical challenge in advancing consideration of OP as a labour force development strategy will be to identify the regions, fisheries, and fleets where it is a positive option, as opposed to the regions, fisheries, and fleets where there may be other ways to achieve the same objectives without the attendant risks.

Chapter 7

OCCUPATIONAL PLURALISM AND THE LABOUR MARKET

Evidence presented in chapter 6 confirms that OP is an established pattern of labour force participation for many fish harvesters and plays an important role in sustaining the workforce. In regions and fleet sectors subject to seasonal constraints on harvesting activities, OP functions as an important source of supplementary income and a means to raise capital for new entrant crew workers who aspire to become owner-operators. Engagement by harvesters in OP also expands and contracts as fishing jobs and incomes are impacted by up-and-down cycles in the fishing economy.

This chapter summarizes evidence on the types of industries and occupations that are most suitable for employment by fish harvesters outside fishing seasons, the current and future availability of jobs in those sectors, the barriers to accessing OP employment opportunities, and how these might be mitigated.

INDUSTRY AND OCCUPATIONAL SECTORS APPROPRIATE FOR FISH HARVESTER OP

The first step in identifying industries and occupations that offer suitable employment opportunities for fish harvesters during non-fishing seasons is to examine past and current employment patterns.

The 2015 CCPFH survey of fish harvesters asked questions about the types of jobs held by fish harvesters outside the fishing industry. In the survey, 22% of Atlantic region and Quebec respondents (captains and crew) reported seasonal employment outside the fishery. Table 7.1 describes the types of jobs those respondents had.[51]

TABLE 7.1 CCPFH 2015 SURVEY, ATLANTIC PROVINCES AND QUEBEC RESPONDENTS, OCCUPATIONS OR INDUSTRIES WHERE THOSE WHO REPORTED WORKING OUTSIDE THEIR PRIMARY FISHING JOBS WERE EMPLOYED		
	Captains (N=176)	Crew (N=83)
Crew member or deckhand, non-fishing vessels	21%	11%
Tourism, related services	6%	25%
Trucking and heavy equipment	22%	5%
Construction trades	17%	7%
Other skilled trades	6%	14%
Agriculture related	6%	7%
Fish processing, handling, buying	12%	4%
Labourer	3%	12%
Boat-building/maintenance	4%	2%
Non-vessel-based seafood and seaweed harvesting (e.g., oysters, clams, rockweed)	NA	14%

Respondents were also asked their views on the types of non-fishing jobs that might be most suitable for fish harvesters who choose to work outside fishing seasons. Note that the findings in table 7.2 came from all respondents, including those who did not engage in OP themselves.

TABLE 7.2 CCPFH 2015 SURVEY, PERCENTAGE OF ATLANTIC PROVINCES AND QUEBEC RESPONDENTS WHO MENTIONED PARTICULAR JOBS/OCCUPATIONS AS SUITABLE FOR OFF-SEASON EMPLOYMENT FOR FISH HARVESTERS

	Captains (N=788)	Crew (N=245)
Skilled trades generally	26%	32%
Construction trades	19%	19%
Trucking and heavy equipment	11%	9%
Labourer	6%	4%
Crew member or deckhand, non-fishing	1%	7%
Tourism, related services	2%	5%

The pattern of responses suggests that construction, skilled trades, and trucking and heavy equipment operation are seen as most suitable for OP employment for fish harvesters.

Statistics Canada tax filer data also provide some evidence on the industries where fish harvesters reported employment earnings outside fishing.[52]

Table 7.3 identifies the industries by province where the greatest numbers of fish harvesters were employed outside their primary fishing jobs. Harvesters generated taxable incomes in many other industries but in much lower numbers than those identified in the table. In Canada overall in 2013, there were about seven thousand wage-earner fish harvesters employed in the industries listed in the table but an equal number across a wide array of other sectors. The key findings are that a few industries tend to employ greater numbers of fish harvesters, but OP employment overall is highly diverse, reflecting local labour market conditions and other factors.

TABLE 7.3 TAX FILER EVIDENCE ON INDUSTRIES WHERE FISH HARVESTERS GENERATED TAXABLE EMPLOYMENT INCOME, 2013

Region	Industries (in order of importance)
Canada	⊗ Construction ⊗ Fish processing ⊗ Wholesale trade ⊗ Public administration ⊗ Agriculture, forestry, and hunting
Newfoundland and Labrador	⊗ Construction ⊗ Fish processing ⊗ Public administration
Nova Scotia	⊗ Fish processing ⊗ Construction ⊗ Wholesale trade
Prince Edward Island	⊗ Wholesale trade ⊗ Agriculture, forestry, and hunting ⊗ Public administration
New Brunswick	⊗ Construction ⊗ Fish processing ⊗ Agriculture, forestry, and hunting
Quebec	⊗ Construction ⊗ Fish processing ⊗ Public administration
Manitoba	⊗ Construction ⊗ Public administration ⊗ Other services
British Columbia	⊗ Construction ⊗ Transportation ⊗ Accommodation and food services

In community case studies carried out for the CCPFH project, participants in interviews and focus groups were asked to identify industries and occupations suitable for fish harvester OP. The report on the Atlantic region case studies summarized the findings as follows:

Jobs that appear to be preferred by many fish harvesters engaging in occupational pluralism include various marine-related jobs that involve working with and on board different kinds of vessels and across fishing enterprises and fisheries, and non-marine-related jobs in carpentry, construction, heavy equipment operation and other types of trades-related work. The availability of those jobs is mixed. Few local jobs apparently exist but carpentry and construction related jobs appear conducive to seasonal and contract work....Fish harvesters have a range of transferable skills, such as carpentry, basic electrical and plumbing skills, and engine repair.[53]

The community studies in Manitoba and British Columbia identified a number of jobs that require skills fish harvesters typically have and that do not conflict with fishing seasons. In Manitoba, key examples were firefighting, forestry work, guide outfitting, seasonal tourism and ecotourism, and construction. Heavy equipment operation and a range of trades were also mentioned, along with fish processing, hatchery work, and fishing gear production.

On North Vancouver Island key sectors were ecotourism and adventure tourism and other marine and fisheries-related activities including guides for sport fishing, vessel maintenance, and fish processing. There were also jobs in aquaculture production and some forestry work, particularly silviculture. In the Prince Rupert region, key sectors identified were the building trades and logging, beachcombing, and salvage work. There was also mention of work in tourism, including ski resorts. Shellfish aquaculture and ocean ranching were seen to have growth potential.

In summary, these findings suggest that fish harvesters engage in a wide diversity of job types reflecting the employment opportunities available during non-fishing seasons in particular regions, but there also appear to be strong preferences for marine-related jobs and trades work. Harvesters naturally gravitate to sectors like tourism, transportation, construction, aquaculture, and fish processing and environmental management that use skills fish harvesters typically have.

There would appear to be good matches for seasonal availability and transferable skills with service industry jobs related to summer or winter tourism (e.g., sport fishing, marine tours, ski resorts), certain government jobs (e.g., snow plowing, road construction) and other fisheries and marine activities (fish handling and processing, ferry operators, fisheries observers, etc.). Construction and related trades, truck transportation, and heavy equipment operation are also regarded as good matches with fish harvesters' skills and lifestyles, and employment opportunities in these jobs may often be available when and where harvesters have time off from fishing.

LABOUR MARKET DEMAND

In considering the encouragement of fish harvester engagement in OP, the next question to be addressed is whether suitable jobs are likely to be available where and when needed.

Employment and Social Development Canada generates labour market forecasts through the Canadian Occupational Projection System (COPS). The system provides ten-year outlooks for job openings by occupation and industry. For the overall Canadian economy, the services sector is projected to dominate job growth, accounting for 88% of total job creation between 2016 and 2026, followed distantly by construction (8%), manufacturing (4%), and the primary sector (0.3%).[54]

Figure 7.1 shows the numbers of job openings by occupation, including new positions and replacements of retirees, that the COPS system anticipates over the 2017–2026 period.[55]

While the great majority of these employment openings will occur

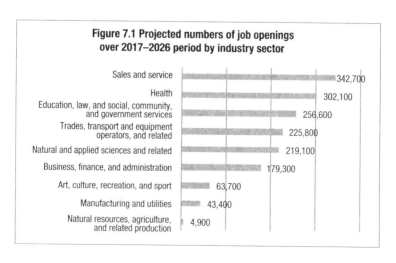

Figure 7.1 Projected numbers of job openings over 2017–2026 period by industry sector

Sales and service	342,700
Health	302,100
Education, law, and social, community, and government services	256,600
Trades, transport and equipment operators, and related	225,800
Natural and applied sciences and related	219,100
Business, finance, and administration	179,300
Art, culture, recreation, and sport	63,700
Manufacturing and utilities	43,400
Natural resources, agriculture, and related production	4,900

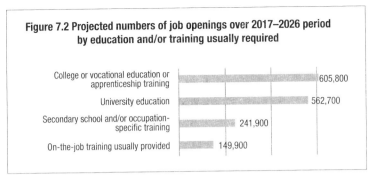

Figure 7.2 Projected numbers of job openings over 2017–2026 period by education and/or training usually required

College or vocational education or apprenticeship training	605,800
University education	562,700
Secondary school and/or occupation-specific training	241,900
On-the-job training usually provided	149,900

in urban communities, it is important to consider that people work and provide services in all these same occupations in rural regions where the anticipated retirement attrition will be higher than in urban areas.

The COPS system also projects employment openings by levels of education and training required, as shown in figure 7.2. Except in the two provinces with fish harvester apprenticeship systems in place (Newfoundland and Labrador and Quebec), the great majority of harvesters would have acquired their knowledge and skills on the job. However, many of the jobs that might suit them for OP employment require college, vocational or apprenticeship qualifications, or other occupation-specific training. This observation reinforces the critical importance of access to appropriate education and training for any strategy to expand OP employment in rural coastal regions.

The COPS system projects 1.6 million job openings in Canada over the 2017–2026 period. Industry expansion (i.e., creation of new positions) is expected to generate 25% of these openings while 75% of all employment opportunities will be replacements for retiring workers and people exiting the labour force for other reasons.

Table 7.4 shows the projected number of job openings in industries where fish harvesters currently find OP employment opportunities according to the research evidence.

TABLE 7.4 CANADA, PROJECTED NUMBERS OF JOB OPENINGS FOR OCCUPATIONS SUITABLE FOR FISH HARVESTER OP EMPLOYMENT, 2017–2026

Transport truck drivers	30,700
Trades helpers and labourers	13,400
Electricians	13,400
Food and beverage servers	11,400
Welders and related machine operators	8,600
Contractors and supervisors, heavy equipment operator crews	8,500
Contractors and supervisors, other construction trades, installers, repairers, and servicers	8,400
Heavy-duty equipment mechanics	7,600
Boat assemblers and inspectors; plastic products assemblers, finishers, and inspectors; industrial painters, coaters, and metal finishing process operators & similar	7,500
Contractors and supervisors, carpentry trades	4,500
Public works maintenance equipment operators and related workers	4,400
Heavy equipment operators	3,600
Process control and machine operators, food, beverage, and related products processing; fish and seafood plant workers and testers and graders	3,500
Residential and commercial installers and servicers	3,200
Construction inspectors	2,300
Carpenters	1,900
Labourers in food, beverage, and related products processing & labourers in fish and seafood processing	1,500
Automotive technicians, mechanics	1,400
Construction millwrights and industrial mechanics	1,000

Again, almost all these occupations will be present in most rural regions where relatively large-scale workforce churn is anticipated due to retirements. Of course, jobs will not be available for every occupation in every community and particularly in remote areas. In addition to access to training, accurate information on where jobs are available and supports for individual and family mobility would be essential elements of any strategy to expand fish harvester engagement in OP.

Service Canada and Employment and Social Development Canada also provide estimates of future job prospects for occupations by province, using a three-point scale of *limited, fair,* and *good.*[56] Table 7.5 identifies occupations that appear to be favoured by fish harvesters for employment outside fishing seasons and that are projected to have "fair" or "good" outlooks for employment opportunities. For illustration purposes, the table covers just three provinces with substantial fisheries, but the types of jobs and anticipated demand levels are very similar for other provinces.

TABLE 7.5 OCCUPATIONAL OUTLOOK FOR JOBS THAT MAY BE SUITABLE FOR FISH HARVESTER OP EMPLOYMENT

Newfoundland and Labrador	
Residential home builders and renovators	Fair
Deck officers, water transport	Fair
Firefighters	Good
Heavy-duty equipment mechanics	Fair
Commercial divers	Fair
Deck crew, water transport	Fair
Aquaculture and marine harvest labourers	Fair
Oil and gas drilling, servicing and related labourers	Fair
Nova Scotia	
Deck officers and crew, water transport	Good
Engineer officers, water transport	Good
Butchers, meat cutters, and fishmongers	Good
Welders and related machine operators	Good

TABLE 7.5 (CONT'D) OCCUPATIONAL OUTLOOK FOR JOBS THAT MAY BE SUITABLE FOR FISH HARVESTER OP EMPLOYMENT

Heavy-duty equipment mechanics	Good
Truck drivers	Good
Plant workers and labourers in fish processing	Good
British Columbia	
Residential home builders and renovators	Good
Tour and travel guides	Good
Heavy-duty equipment mechanics	Good
Commercial divers	Good
Truck drivers	Good
Heavy equipment operators	Fair
Officers & crew, water transport, boat and cable ferry operators, related occupations	Fair
Construction trades helpers and labourers	Fair
Logging machinery operators	Good

These outlooks again confirm positive job prospects in occupations that appear to be suitable employment for fish harvesters during non-fishing seasons.

BARRIERS TO OP

In the 2015 CCPFH survey, harvesters who did not earn employment income outside their fishing jobs identified barriers to their participation in OP. The most frequently mentioned issues were lack of available jobs locally, family and financial constraints on leaving home areas for work, lack of qualifications to access other jobs, and age-related factors. Three of these are potentially mitigated through policy and program interventions. These findings also suggest that a strategy to expand OP should focus primarily on younger fisheries workers and new entrants.

The report on the community case studies in the Atlantic provinces drew the following conclusions on constraints and supports for OP.

The most significant barrier is the lack of reasonably well-paid local em-
ployment opportunities suitable for harvesters and that offer employment
outside the fishing season or [that] can be done during the season as with
harvesters who invest in bed and breakfasts or restaurants for the tourism
trade.

There are a number of family issues that appear to enable or impede
occupational pluralism. Young fish harvesters appear more likely to have
an incentive to gain well-paying job opportunities outside the fishing
season, partly because of financial needs related to household and family
expenses and the costs associated with buying their own enterprise.…

Fish harvesters seeking off-season employment would benefit from
innovative recognition of existing skills and building on those to develop
and acquire additional training. Enhanced information campaigns about
training opportunities and job opportunities would help this process, as
well as new training initiatives and financial resources. New and en-
hanced labour market information could be developed through improved
relationships and coordination among public and private regional bodies
and communicated through new media platforms, including new websites
and fish harvester-driven social media sites.[57]

As noted above, community stakeholders from outside the fishing industry were receptive to OP strategies to address wider demographic and labour-supply challenges. Some identified the need for
improved labour market information (LMI) and more effective labour
market planning.

The challenge of attaining better labour market information was identified
implicitly or explicitly as an area needing attention. In Nova Scotia, for
example, officials working with a regional economic development orga-
nization have been struggling to track movements of labour from one
industry to another. This information is critical for understanding what
sectors need labour and when labour is needed. Coordination among gov-
ernmental and non-governmental organizations around labour market
information resources and needs might help in the area.

For fish harvesters interested in occupational pluralism, better information is needed about the dynamics of opportunities in other sectors. For example, one challenge the processing sector in Southwest Nova Scotia has, as identified by an economic development official collaborating with the sector, is getting a clearer picture of when the labour needs occur throughout the year as production ebbs and flows. Coordination might also help improve the sharing of existing labour market information....A coordinated approach around labour market information could ensure that such information is shared with relevant groups.[58]

The community case study in Quebec encountered a similar pattern: industry participants tended to see less need for OP and to emphasize the lack of suitable employment options, while community leaders and economic development officials more readily identified opportunities to address wider demographic and labour supply challenges through OP strategies.

In Manitoba, many harvesters live and work in isolated and fly-in communities where there are few employment opportunities outside

(CCPFH)

the fishery. Training is very expensive because of costs related to travel and living away from home, and the same constraints apply for travel to access non-fishing jobs.

In British Columbia key informants again identified the need to know more about available job and training opportunities. The fishers' EI system in British Columbia does not support training for fish harvesters as much as in eastern Canada, and in general does not fund training for non-fishing activities for harvesters. Stakeholders identified the need for a program that helps them identify and match harvester skills with job opportunities or self-employment options. For example, there are local shortages of small machinery repair technicians and marine insurance brokers, both jobs that harvesters could learn to do if they had access to appropriate training.

Some harvesters in British Columbia want to use their vessels for ecotourism businesses but were constrained by issues with insurance for carrying passengers. Also, because they cannot have fishing gear in the water during the off-season, they cannot do demonstrations for tourists. Participants also described the reluctance of harvesters to change their work patterns for fear of losing access to EI to fall back on if self-employment ventures did not work out. It was suggested that community leadership and innovative programming efforts are required to convince people that they can try new things and get the training support and financial security they need to take risks.

As noted above, respondents in the 2015 CCPFH survey of captains and crew workers in the Atlantic region and Quebec expressed positive views on the potential value of expanded OP as a way for the industry to attract and retain new entrants. Figure 7.3 shows the pattern of responses on how helpful certain types of interventions might be in supporting and encouraging OP.

On a scale of one to five, from *not helpful at all* (1) to *very helpful* (5), all the suggested options were scored positively, with the strongest emphasis on information about job opportunities and training.[59] Crew respondents were generally more positive than captains about the

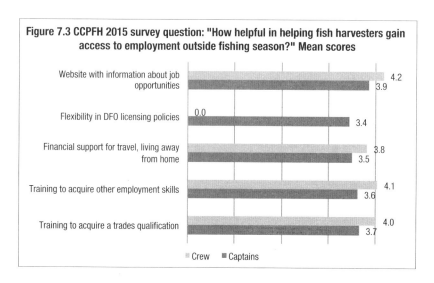

Figure 7.3 CCPFH 2015 survey question: "How helpful in helping fish harvesters gain access to employment outside fishing season?" Mean scores

efficacy of these approaches, perhaps because they might have more to gain from such interventions and supports.

On a separate, open-ended survey question, captain and crew interviewees were asked to identify the types of skills training that would be most useful and relevant for fish harvesters wanting to engage in OP. Figure 7.4 shows the types of skills training most frequently mentioned by the fish harvester respondents in the Atlantic region and Quebec. (There were no notable differences in responses from captain and crew respondents.)

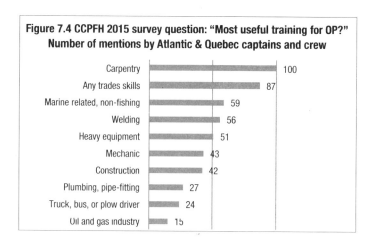

Figure 7.4 CCPFH 2015 survey question: "Most useful training for OP?" Number of mentions by Atlantic & Quebec captains and crew

THE TAKEAWAYS

As discussed in chapter 6, OP is not a necessary or attractive option for all harvesters in all regions and fleet sectors. There are fisheries that provide more or less year-round employment and fully adequate incomes, and there are opportunities to develop more such fisheries through fleet restructuring and innovations in fisheries management policies and practices. But there will still be fishing regions and fleets where climate and resource constraints limit fishing activities to more or less limited seasons.

The evidence from survey research, community consultations, and tax filer data indicates that fish harvesters who engage in OP employment find jobs in a diverse range of industries and occupations reflecting local labour market conditions, transferability of job skills, and individual preferences. However, there clearly are industry sectors where fish harvesters more often find OP employment, including construction and other skilled trades, crewing on non-fishing vessels and other marine activities, and machinery and equipment operation.

The available labour market forecasts suggest that there will be significant demand for new labour supply in many of the occupations and industry sectors where fish harvesters currently pursue OP activities. Many of these jobs are typically present in rural regions and in industries with some degree of seasonality.

Perhaps the most significant factor identified in the COPS labour market outlook is that upwards of 75% of job opportunities in the Canadian economy overall will be generated by workforce attrition through retirement and other factors. Data on demographic trends confirm that worker retirements in rural industries and occupations will be much higher than for the economy overall, perhaps as high as 40% attrition by 2025; therefore, innovative approaches to sharing available labour supply among different sectors will be a priority for planners and decision-makers in all sectors, not just in the fishery. In short, despite common perceptions among fish harvesters that non-fishing employment opportunities are scarce, there is solid evidence to suggest that job availability for them will improve and will not be a fundamental or unmanageable constraint on expanded engagement in OP.

The most significant barriers to expanded fish harvester participation in OP have been identified as a lack of information about available jobs, lack of access to relevant and affordable training, the costs and family pressures arising from travel to access jobs or participate in training, and rigidities and disincentives in the EI system. To overcome these barriers and constraints, the key areas for intervention would appear to be more effective LMI tools, improved access to education and training programs for bridging to non-fishing jobs, services to recognize and certify fish harvesters' transferable job skills, and improved financial supports for labour mobility and access to training.

Two higher-level findings are noteworthy. First, there is a high level of receptivity among leaders and officials in local government, economic development agencies, and the training sector to exploring OP as part of a wider strategy to address looming labour shortages in rural economies, and a willingness to consider new approaches to facilitating cross-sector sharing of labour supply in seasonal industries.

Second, the EI system looms large as a stabilizer of the seasonal fisheries labour force but also as both a facilitator and a constraint for labour mobility and OP. Fish harvesters express concern that greater participation in OP may jeopardize their access to EI or, indeed, may encourage government to pursue further cuts in the fishers' EI program. By the same token, harvesters also identify ways the EI system could provide more effective support for OP in terms of access to training and support for geographic mobility. These issues are examined in greater depth in the next chapter.

Chapter 8

EMPLOYMENT INSURANCE AND OCCUPATIONAL PLURALISM

A *s discussed, it is in the nature of the fishing industry that most harvesters* receive no income from fishing during lengthy periods every year. According to census data, a quarter or more of fish harvesters in Canada and almost one-third in Newfoundland and Labrador and Quebec were active in their fishing jobs for only thirteen weeks or less in 2016. Over two-thirds of Canadian harvesters work in the industry for half the year or less. Using census data, figure 8.1 shows the levels of seasonality for four provinces and nationally for "fishermen/-women" in 2016. Nova Scotia and British Columbia have the most harvesters employed in fishing for half the year or more, but in both cases more than half work for six months or less.

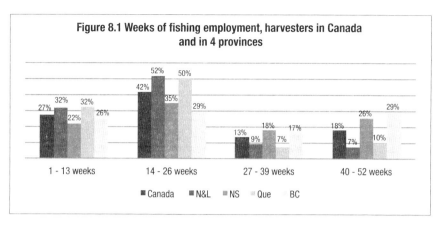

Figure 8.1 Weeks of fishing employment, harvesters in Canada and in 4 provinces

In addition to its seasonality, the fishing industry is also subject to cycles in resource abundance and market demand. Over the 2000–2017 period fish harvester incomes were depressed for several years before growing to record highs, due largely to macro-economic factors beyond industry control. In figure 8.2, using tax filer data, average pre-tax and after-inflation fishing incomes for harvesters in Canada are indexed to the year 2000.

The socio-economic sustainability of the fishery—as with other important seasonal industries—has long required that workers have sources of supplementary income during non-working periods and some protection against industry downturns. For committed professional fish harvesters—enterprise owners and crew workers—there have been two primary sources of such income that have sustained their attachment to the industry: OP and EI.

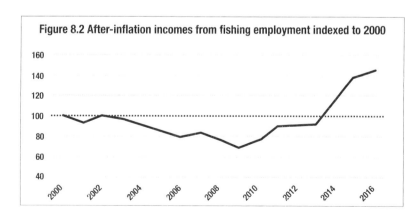

Figure 8.2 After-inflation incomes from fishing employment indexed to 2000

There is long-standing debate, and conflicting evidence, on whether access to EI suppresses or facilitates fish harvester engagement in OP. Mainstream economists generally support the view that if EI did not "subsidize" their unemployment, workers in high unemployment regions would migrate to stronger labour markets and—deprived of low-cost labour—industries like the fisheries would have to restructure to be less seasonal and more efficient and productive. A prominent business columnist in the *Globe and Mail* captures this argument succinctly: "Meanwhile, the government is pledging to make changes to EI....Under the current system, people in high unemployment regions have to work less to earn maximum benefits, creating a disincentive to work more than the minimum, or to move in search of work."[60]

The counter-argument is that worker mobility is structurally constrained by demographic factors, education and training deficits, by the high costs of training and relocation, and, most often, by the lack of demand in accessible labour markets. If EI were less available the outcome would almost certainly be greater poverty for substantial rural populations that lack mobility and, over time, significant shrinkage in the labour supply for industries that, by their nature, are seasonal. There is also convincing evidence that, rather than discouraging OP, EI actually facilitates it by providing a safety net and access to training and adjustment benefits and by creating incentives for recipients to take advantage of short-term employment opportunities.

Overall, findings from the CCPFH FLMI study suggest that such debates may in fact be losing relevance. Current economic and demographic trends call for new ideas on how to align the EI system more effectively with wider strategies to advance sustainable development in regions that depend on seasonal industries. Three socio-economic shifts suggest the need for and timeliness of a serious re-examination of the relationship between OP and EI in the fish harvesting sector: the sustained and significant rise in fish harvester incomes; accelerating retirement attrition in the fishing labour force; and looming labour shortages across other rural seasonal industries and occupations.

For decades, an oversupply of labour in rural coastal labour markets has reinforced reliance on EI and its earlier iteration, UI. To the extent that rural economies will for the foreseeable future be grappling with labour shortages, there are compelling reasons to explore new ways to support OP employment and new policy objectives for the EI system.

This all leads to an obvious and simple conclusion: if we are to keep building a successful fishing industry producing high-quality food products and generating major export earnings, we have to figure out how to sustain a skilled and committed labour force that is well-adapted to seasonal work and uneven income cycles over the work year. In this chapter, we explore these issues and identify possible innovations in EI policies to support attraction and retention of new labour supply in the fishing industry.

EI AND THE FISHERIES LABOUR MARKET

As discussed in chapter 7, the advent of UI after the Second World War made it possible for seasonal industries to retain labour supply and helped bring rural communities out of poverty. Changes to the UI Act in 1956 provided eligibility for fish harvesters—the first and still the only group of self-employed workers to be covered.[61]

There can be no question that UI—and since 1996, EI—have been foundational for the fishing industry as it operates in Canada. In the 2015 CCPFH survey, 88% of captains and 93% of crew respondents in the Atlantic provinces and Quebec reported having qualified for EI benefits in the previous twelve months. Of this population, 89% of captains, and 67% of crew qualified under the EI fishing benefits program while the remainder were covered by regular EI.

Statistics Canada tax filer data provides further evidence on the role of EI in stabilizing the fish harvester labour force. Figure 8.3 shows the trends for average after-inflation fishing and EI incomes for fish harvesters during the 2000–2016 period in Canada.

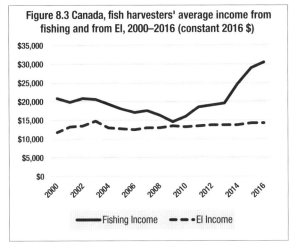

Figure 8.3 Canada, fish harvesters' average income from fishing and from EI, 2000–2016 (constant 2016 $)

Fishing Income ——— EI Income ---

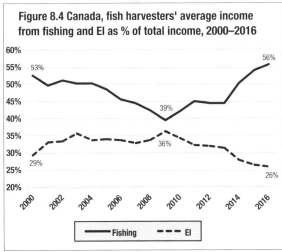

Figure 8.4 Canada, fish harvesters' average income from fishing and EI as % of total income, 2000–2016

Fishing ——— EI ---

As figure 8.3 shows, EI provided stability for fish harvesters over a period characterized by sharp ups and downs in employment incomes. It is also evident that average EI income did not vary a great deal from year to year over the period in constant dollar terms, with a 33% increase in after-inflation dollars (2016) over the seventeen years.

Figure 8.4 shows changes in average fish harvesters' incomes received from fishing employment and EI benefits as percentages of total pretax, after-inflation income from all sources over the 2000–2016 period.[62] This again confirms the role of EI in stabilizing incomes through the major downturn in the industry during the 2007–2009 recession.

There were significant variations in the impacts of EI income across regions. Figures 8.5 and 8.6 compare average incomes for harvesters from fishing employment and EI benefits at the lowest point in the economic downturn in 2009 and after the recovery in 2016.

In 2009, average EI income actually exceeded fishing income in provinces other than Nova Scotia and British Columbia, in the latter

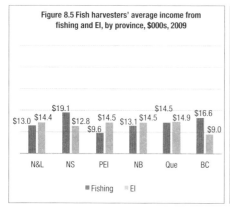

Figure 8.5 Fish harvesters' average income from fishing and EI, by province, $000s, 2009

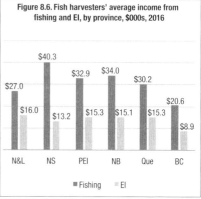

Figure 8.6. Fish harvesters' average income from fishing and EI, by province, $000s, 2016

case because EI income is atypically low. This situation persisted over three years (2008–2010), suggesting that the stability of the labour force and the viability of many fishing enterprises might have been in jeopardy over that period were it not for EI benefits.

In 2016, after full recovery from the Great Recession, EI benefit incomes had increased marginally in most provinces, but fishing incomes were up substantially over 2009 in every province except British Columbia.

EI FISHING BENEFITS

There are three sub-programs within the EI system that are relevant to this discussion: regular benefits for eligible workers in any industry sector, fishing benefits available only to eligible self-employed fish harvesters, and what are known as Part 2 benefits that cover training costs and other supports for finding and keeping employment. The total costs of the three programs in fiscal year 2017–2018 are shown in table 8.1.[63]

TABLE 8.1 TOTAL EI EXPENDITURES ON REGULAR BENEFITS, FISHING BENEFITS, AND PART 2 BENEFITS, FISCAL YEAR 2017–2018	
Regular EI benefits	$11,751 million
Fishing EI benefits	$327 million
Part 2 EI benefits and support measures	$2,168 million

The EI fishing benefits program applies to self-employed fish harvesters, including captains and crew members, who receive income through catch shares rather than regular wages.[64] The key differences between fishing benefits and regular benefits are that eligibility is determined by earnings, not hours, and there are two possible claim periods within a year.

To be eligible for EI fishing benefits a harvester must be self-employed and involved in making the catch and related activities. The qualifying period for fishing earnings is thirty-one weeks before the benefit period, which can start in the week of October 1 for a winter claim based on summer fishing, or in the week of March 1 for a summer claim based on winter fishing. It is possible to establish two claims a year if a harvester fishes in both seasons with periods of unemployment in between.

As with regular benefits, the amount of work needed to qualify for benefits varies depending on the unemployment rate in the EI Economic Region. Harvesters need earnings from fishing ranging from $2,500 to $4,200, depending on the local unemployment rate ($2,500 applies with an unemployment rate of more than 13%, and $4,200 applies when the unemployment rate is less than 6%). The rationale for regionally variable entrance requirements (VER) in EI is that workers are more likely to lose jobs and have difficulty finding new ones in areas of higher unemployment.

Double claims are more common in some fisheries and regions than in others. In 2014, 40% of harvesters made both summer and winter claims, and 98% of such claims were in the Atlantic provinces and Quebec. Almost half (47%) of harvesters have only a summer claim. Thus, the EI eligibility rules play out differently in different types of fisheries and in different regions of the country. Harvesters who can make two claims are likely fishing actively for more than half the year and therefore may have less need or incentive to take on non-fishing work in the off months. But the opportunity to make double claims may also create incentives for enterprise owner-operators to diversify their fishing activities to extend their seasons, and incentives for crew to find work in different fishing enterprises over the course of the year. Put simply, in some industry situations fishers' EI generates incentives for greater OP *within* the fishery.

Rules on suitable employment and reasonable job search apply to all claimants, including those on fishing benefits. Fish harvesters are obligated to look for and accept suitable work in fishing, or fisheries-related training, but not necessarily other types of work. This does not prevent them from accepting other types of work, but if they work sufficient hours to establish a regular EI claim, they lose eligibility for fishing benefits on their next EI claim. Harvesters can work part-time at non-fishing work while receiving fishing benefits.

For all EI income benefits, the basic formula is 55% of average insurable weekly earnings up to a maximum level. For 2018, maximum insurable earnings were $51,700. This means that a harvester can receive a maximum amount of $547 per week on EI (55% of $51,700 divided by 52). Some three-quarters of fish harvester claimants receive maximum benefits compared to about half of regular claimants, and their average benefit is higher than for regular EI claimants. This suggests that harvesters might not want to take on non-fishing employment that would require them to shift to regular benefits. If maximum benefits are achieved solely with fishing earnings, the incentive to take on additional work is reduced, especially low-wage work that would pay less than EI benefits.

Given a choice, it seems that most crew members opt for fishing benefits if they can qualify. The fixed duration results in a longer benefit period than would apply with a regular EI claim after a short fishing season. As mentioned, fishing benefits are particularly attractive in situations where double claims are possible.

REGULAR EI

While the great majority of fish harvesters in Canada qualify under the fishers' EI program, there is a trend in recent years for more harvesters to transfer to the regular EI program. Among other things, this reflects the fact that increasing numbers of enterprise owners have been incorporating for tax purposes and paying themselves and their crews regular wages rather than catch shares.

Since the 1996 reform of the UI program, eligibility for regular benefits has been based on the sum of all hours of work during a fifty-two-week qualifying period. This approach encourages multiple job holding and OP, as there are no minimum hours per job, and every hour counts. This benefits many seasonal workers who often work long hours for only a few weeks. For example, fish processing plants will operate 24-7 with extra shifts to handle heavy initial landings during the opening weeks of the lobster and snow crab fisheries, but then production usually falls off for the remainder of the season.

The VERs are a major factor in determining eligibility for regular EI. The number of hours of work needed to qualify for benefits ranges from 420 in a region with an unemployment rate over 13% to 700 in a region with a rate of 6% or less. The same basic formula applies for regular claimants as for EI fishing benefits claimants: 55% of average insurable weekly earnings, maximum insurable earnings of $51,700, and maximum weekly EI benefit of $547.

The range of weeks that one can collect regular benefits is between 14 and 45. If a harvester only has the minimum hours (420) needed to qualify in a region of high unemployment, the duration ranges from twenty-six to thirty-two weeks. With only the minimum 700 hours needed to qualify in a region with the lowest unemployment rate (<6%) the claim duration would be only fourteen weeks. Only in regions with more than 10% unemployment could claimants get the full forty-five weeks of benefits.

Regular EI beneficiaries are required to search for and accept "suitable employment." Rule changes introduced in 2013 required "frequent claimants"—which includes most seasonal workers—to accept "any work you are qualified to perform" after six weeks on EI, at 80% to 70% percent of their normal wage, and that was within a daily commute of up to one hour. The government explicitly linked this change

(CCPFH)

to a policy goal of reducing the need for food processing plants to bring temporary foreign workers into regions with high unemployment. This is an example of using EI rules as "sticks" to force participation in OP. Employers expressed concerns that the provisions might exacerbate local labour shortages by discouraging people from staying in the region. In 2016 the government removed these requirements.

The rules for regular EI impact OP strategies among fisheries workers, other seasonal workers, and employers in diverse ways. In terms of encouraging OP, the use of "best weeks" is an improvement,[65] but the formula remains challenging for many seasonal workers, especially those in lower unemployment regions. It is still more of a "stick" than a "carrot" and does not relate to the actual weeks of work available in their primary job.

EI pilot projects have succeeded in encouraging more work time for recipients by reducing the amount of clawback of earnings from occasional jobs while receiving EI benefits. However, there is anecdotal evidence that this approach may create unintended incentives for employers to lay off workers once they qualify for EI, then bring them back on an as-needed basis to reduce overall labour costs.

Since EI does not cover self-employment activities other than for fish harvesters there is a definite disincentive for unemployed people to pursue self-employment options. The lack of coverage may also encourage underreporting of income and participation in underground economy activities.

PART 2 EI BENEFITS AND PROGRAMS

Part 2 of the EI Act provides for the Employment Benefits and Support Measures. Benefits include skills training, wage subsidies, and self-employment assistance, while support measures are employment assistance services such as job counselling. Labour Market Development Agreements are negotiated with each province governing how the EI Part 2 funds are spent. Current claimants can receive income benefits and access to Employment Benefits and Support Measures, while former claimants (within three years of a claim) can access only Employment Benefits and Support Measures programs. Job seekers who have never qualified for EI only have access to certain general support measures such as job counselling.

Because EI-funded programs are delivered provincially, there are differences in the opportunities seasonal workers may have to access training and other supports. Most training seems to be aimed at getting people into long-term primary jobs rather than preparing people for work in two or more seasonal occupations within an OP strategy. For fishers' EI claimants, training options may be limited to fisheries-related programs. An alternative approach might be to help seasonal workers acquire a mix of skills appropriate to a seasonal economy, which would be supportive of occupational or geographical mobility.

Part 2 Employment Benefits and Support Measures also offer support through training and income benefits for EI claimants to develop their own businesses. However, once a business is started, self-employed owners are no longer eligible for EI. This again raises the issue of whether eligibility for EI benefits might be extended to seasonally self-employed people as part of an OP strategy.

INTERNATIONAL COMPARISONS

Canadian EI benefit rates are considerably lower than those in many other countries, particularly Nordic countries with similar patterns of seasonal employment. In these systems the benefit rate is often in the range of 70–90% of earnings—90% in Denmark, 80% in Sweden and Switzerland—compared to 55% in Canada. Like Canada, most countries have maximum insurable earnings. The United Kingdom and Ireland have a flat rate benefit, while a few others use a combination of a standard amount tied to average wages and a basic benefit with a top-up based on earnings.

An Organisation for Economic Co-operation and Development (OECD) study showed that for the first year of unemployment, Canada has a net earnings replacement rate above the OECD average but below the rate of many other developed countries including Finland, Germany, France, Spain, Belgium, Norway, Netherlands, Portugal, and Switzerland.[66] However, Canada's access criteria are relatively more favourable for seasonal workers: most countries base eligibility on days, weeks, or months of work, whereas in Canada it is based on hours or, in the case of EI fishing benefits, earnings.

Many countries also adjust duration of benefits by age. Duration is usually shorter for younger workers, and participation in labour market programs may be mandatory, while older workers have longer duration of benefits without such requirements. In the case of Sweden, duration is higher for those with dependent children.

Countries that allow working while collecting unemployment benefits have a formula for disregarding some dollar amounts or portion of earnings, similar to Canada's approach. For example, Finland reduces benefits by 50% of earnings above a flat earnings exemption; the recipient cannot make more on benefits and earnings than their original earnings on which the claim was based. Austria and Germany ignore a small amount of earnings but end the entitlement if earnings exceed that minimum, which creates a strong disincentive for pursuing additional part-time or occasional employment opportunities. Sweden allows the person to retain benefits if the new job has fewer hours than the original job, providing benefits for the difference in hours. This approach makes it relatively easy for a seasonal worker to work part-time in the off-season without losing benefits. Several countries are testing policies to allow both work and benefits to maintain a work incentive. This would be helpful in developing a strategy to facilitate OP for seasonal workers.

ALIGNING EI POLICIES WITH OP STRATEGIES

Important changes have been made to EI in Canada to better suit seasonal workers. Examples include dropping the "intensity" rule, which reduced benefits for frequent users; moving to a "best weeks" formula for calculating benefit rates; improving the incentive to work while on claim; and most recently, eliminating onerous new entrant and re-entrant eligibility requirements for both regular and fishing benefits. Nevertheless, further changes could help to improve the fit between EI and the labour market realities for fish harvesters and other seasonal workers and employers.[67] The goal would be to improve flexibility and incentives for individuals and households to put together livelihoods or create jobs, and in doing so, to facilitate greater participation in OP.

The formula for calculating benefits could be adjusted to remove the remaining penalties for fluctuating work and earnings, and the formula should be neutral with respect to the timing of work. While the use of variable best weeks is good, having a minimum number of weeks to calculate benefits can still affect the EI benefit rate for some patterns of work. The use of a best weeks approach in Canada (based on weeks, not hours) is unique and impacts the effective income replacement rate for seasonal workers who work long hours during short fishing seasons.

Measures to make working while on claim more rewarding are a positive way to support OP. Additional work should not jeopardize the future EI eligibility or make claimants worse off or negatively impact a future claim. It should be possible to design a formula that works for everyone and is transparent, perhaps with a higher dollar threshold for ignoring occasional earnings while on claim and a percentage scale above that.

For fish harvesters, there are additional considerations around maintaining fishing status that need to be reviewed. For example, the requirement to be available while on claim for any fishing work is problematic from an OP perspective. Several countries with similar seasonal industries are exploring more effective ways to combine unemployment benefits with work to encourage greater participation in OP.

On a wider front, EI coverage could be extended to other seasonally self-employed workers. There is currently no equivalent to EI fishing benefits for loggers or farmers or small tourist operators. Fishing benefits and special benefits for self-employed individuals provide models that could be adapted for more general applications or for particular sectors.[68] The inclusion of self-employed workers is the norm in many comparable countries with similar labour markets (e.g., Nordic countries), and so there are tested models that could be adapted to Canadian circumstances. Expanding EI coverage to self-employed workers in other industries could help create a new seasonal labour market environment in which individuals move more easily and confidently from one sector to another over the year. It could also help reduce underground economic activities in sectors like homebuilding, vessel maintenance, and auto repair.

EI could better recognize combinations of paid work and self-employment that are reflective of local labour markets in rural regions. Currently, earnings from paid work can be added to fish harvesters' insurable earnings. This is also the case for those claiming special benefits as self-employed. This is not an option for regular claimants. Additionally, fishing claimants cannot count non-fishing self-employed earnings. A flexible program design where eligibility and benefits are based on all income-generating work could be considered. A related consideration would be to allow the option to choose between fishing and regular EI, where a fish harvester engages in both fishing and non-fishing work. Finally, given the specific employment challenges facing seasonal workers, ways of smoothing income gaps could be considered. The longer reference period in many countries is another way to add flexibility around ensuring entitlements for various patterns of work.

With regard to special benefits, eligibility could be adjusted to better reflect the more limited hours available for seasonal workers. The current minimum of 600 hours is beyond the hours worked during full-time employment for a three-month contract.

EI could be used to help older workers in fishing and other seasonal industries ease out of the labour force. In physically demanding industries like the fisheries, workers often find it difficult to keep up as they get older. They may incur greater risks to health and safety by trying to maintain their incomes until they reach eligibility for Old Age Security and the Canada Pension Plan income. Providing financial support for older harvesters to help them transition out of the fishery could help make more enterprises available to new entrants and perhaps reduce upward pressures on licence prices. Other countries have developed ways to address this challenge. Australia, for instance, has a part-time allowance for older workers, while Denmark has an early retirement scheme featuring entitlement to flexible employment, with benefits of 91–100% of the maximum rates.

OP could take a different form for older workers, facilitated by extended, flexible income benefits through EI until pension entitlement age is reached. This could be integrated with an early retirement program that would allow aging workers in physically demanding seasonal work to stay in their homes and communities, leading the way for younger people to find work and help employers renew the workforce. Governments could partner with employers and unions in the design and funding of such early retirement programs.

EI Part 2 employment support measures could do more to support participation in OP by workers in seasonal industries. The goal would be to promote the attractiveness of seasonal jobs to benefit families, employers, and communities as well as address the labour shortages that threaten like fisheries, agriculture, tourism, and other sectors. A "carrot" approach that enhances skills and allows flexible packaging of jobs and income support may be more effective than more "sticks" to force EI recipients to take any available jobs just to get them off the program.

Most Nordic countries have more active labour market programming than Canada, while also providing higher benefits. Countries are using positive labour market services and supports to reduce reliance on unemployment insurance programs, far exceeding what is done in Canada. Flexibility is needed to tailor training and other supports to the available work opportunities to allow workers to stay in seasonal industries and communities, including temporary mobility for jobs in the off-season.

The EI fishing benefits program is the closest thing in Canada to such a targeted program. However, greater flexibility is key. In fishing, for example, predictable non-fishing periods and opportunities for non-fishing work in the off-season differ among regions. EI could work with this variability more effectively and become a more dynamic program. This could include more flexible program parameters as well as more personalized employment supports. However, the latter is a challenge given that face-to-face interactions between EI officials and clients have been reduced in the administration of the Canada's EI program.

For fish harvesters, the impact of EI rules and fisheries management policies on the cycles of work and unemployment continue to be the primary concern. Still, in regions with restricted fishing seasons the challenges harvesters face when trying to mix fishing with other kinds of income-generating work deserve almost equal attention.

For plant workers and their employers, changing EI in ways that enable local workers, including immigrants with permanent residence status, to have more rewarding livelihoods is the only real alternative to continued reliance on temporary foreign workers. For both harvesters and plant workers, EI can play a critically important role in facilitating generational transition and workforce renewal.

Many countries take a more life-cycle approach to unemployment insurance programming. There are active labour market measures for young people to help them establish themselves, followed by enhanced benefits for prime-age workers with dependent children and provisions for older workers that are integrated with public pension systems. There are also measures to facilitate older workers' smooth withdrawal from the labour force. Such a policy approach could help to address the challenges identified for fishery workers and other seasonal industries in Canada.

POLICY PERSPECTIVE ON EI AND OP

Prominent Canadian economist Dr. Frances Woolley encapsulates the traditional policy debate on EI in a recent article.

> *Any policy maker whose sole aim was to create a plan to insure workers against job loss would never have come up with our present system. Which raises the question: why do we have the system we do?*
>
> *There are some cynical, and not entirely inaccurate answers: EI is for winning votes in Atlantic Canada. EI is for making depressed regions of the country economically viable; for keeping small communities alive. EI is for subsidizing industries that are, for one reason or another, considered to be important to the Canadian economy, like the fisheries. Yet these answers raise the question, Why EI? Why use EI for regional subsidies, rather than another scheme, such as equalization?*[69]

Along with many other economists—particularly those in regions of Canada where low unemployment and full-time, full-year jobs are the norm—Dr. Woolley takes it as obvious that a well-structured and properly managed EI system would focus primarily on insuring workers against occasional loss of employment, leaving regional development and industrial strategies to other purpose-built policies and programs. She specifically calls for "some kind of brake on the subsidies EI delivers to the fishing and construction industries."

The evidence reviewed above confirms how important the EI system and its diverse array of services have been for the Canadian fishing industry. Without it, it is hard to imagine that the fisheries could have maintained a labour force over the past fifty years. Some might argue that Canada could benefit without the industry as it is currently structured, or at least without much of its rural coastal population base. But the question is academic.

Any initiative to change and improve the industry must consider its status today: a predominance of small, owner-operator enterprises and self-employed workers, seasonal employment, and reliance on EI for income stabilization. For the last fifty years, fisheries-dependent regions were characterized by an oversupply of labour. The UI and EI systems supplemented employment income for workers whose employers and industries could not provide sufficient annual earnings to sustain them in place. People who took up and remained in these jobs chose to live on marginal incomes in their home communities as preferable to perhaps more stressful urban poverty. These realities must be considered in thinking about possible reforms to the EI system as part of wider strategies to attract and retain new labour supply for rural seasonal industries.

For all intents and purposes, the EI fishing benefits program has functioned as a guaranteed annual income tailored to sustain and support this particular industry as it grapples with the limits of seasonal employment and the occasionally sharp reversals in the fishing economy. The same could be said of the impacts of regular EI for frequent users in seasonal industries like fish plants and summer tourism operations. To the extent that socio-economic sustainability and labour force stability were the goals in these sectors, the EI program has been largely successful.

Evidence compiled by the CCPFH FLMI report suggests that labour market conditions in rural coastal regions are in sharp transition. As a result, EI may now need to evolve to keep pace, presenting an opportune time for the basic reconsideration of EI policy objectives and the program's role in sustaining rural seasonal industries. We now face a future in which, in the fish harvesting sector, many employers will be able to pay more competitive wages or crew shares and will increasingly do so to attract and retain the new entrants needed from outside their normal catchment areas. But many, if not most, fish harvesting jobs will still be seasonal, and many, if not most, harvesters will still have six months or more each year with no employment income from fishing. Even with higher fishing incomes, efforts by employers, by industry organizations, and by government agencies to attract and retain new labour supply will need to manage the seasonality challenge.

With accelerating labour shortages across many other industry sectors within rural regions, expanded and modernized OP may be an important avenue for labour force renewal in the fisheries. If so, innovations in EI policies and programs will likely be integral to such a strategy.

In future, the encouragement of expanded OP may not require more "sticks and carrots" in terms of EI penalties and incentives. The major reason why more and more fish harvesters, particularly young new entrants, may choose to pursue OP more than in the past is because it works economically and can help them launch successful fishing careers. Table 8.2 shows average non-fishing employment income for those fish harvesters who participated in OP and compares percentage changes in EI benefit income and OP employment income over the 2000–2016 period.

TABLE 8.2 AVERAGE NON-FISHING (OP) EMPLOYMENT AND EI INCOME FOR FISH HARVESTERS IN 2016, AND PERCENTAGE CHANGE IN OP AND EI INCOME IN AFTER-INFLATION DOLLARS, 2009–2016				
	Income 2016		% Change 2009–2016	
	Non-fishing Jobs	EI Benefits	Non-fishing Jobs (%)	EI Benefits (%)
Newfoundland and Labrador	$21,509	$15,966	+ 43	+ 11
Prince Edward Island	$17,213	$15,315	+ 12	+ 6
Nova Scotia	$20,054	$13,208	+ 21	+ 4
New Brunswick	$17,233	$15,135	+ 3	+ 4
Quebec	$15,394	$15,302	+ 10	+ 3
British Columbia	$24,470	$8,919	+ 7	-1
Canada	$20,903	$14,124	+ 13	+ 6

This tax filer data confirms that, with some regional variations, most fish harvesters who engaged in non-fishing OP employment generated average incomes substantially higher than average EI incomes, and over the 2009–2016 period OP income grew more strongly in after-inflation terms than EI income—more than twice the rate of growth in Canada overall.[70]

Perhaps the most effective ways to encourage greater OP employment—and as a consequence, less reliance on EI—is to make younger fish harvesters more aware of employment opportunities and earning potential, and to build more on-ramps with training programs, LMI services, and supports for mobility and family adjustment.

Chapter 9

UNDERPERFORMANCE IN THE BRITISH COLUMBIA FISHERY

The picture of the Canadian fisheries that emerges from the previous chapters is of an industry with important potential for sustainable economic success but with serious challenges on the labour market side. However, the fishery in British Columbia does not fit this picture: it has the same challenges but not, it seems, the improving economic trends for the fish harvesting sector and fishing communities.

Comprised of 2,400 small and medium-sized businesses employing just over 5,700 harvesters, the commercial fishery is a small part of the British Columbia economy overall. Nevertheless, it has significant advantages compared to other fishing regions. Unlike the industry in Atlantic Canada, the British Columbia fishery has ready access to millions of urban consumers within the province and in the US northwest, and has strong transportation and business links with surging markets in Asia. Historically, the British Columbia industry grew wealthy on seasonal salmon runs, but today's salmon fisheries are scaled back to a fraction of past levels with uncertain landings from year to year. However, British Columbia's groundfish and shellfish fisheries are healthy and are earning record high prices in local and export markets.

But the overall economic performance of British Columbia fisheries is shaky, the result it seems of a unique industry structure and a DFO policy environment that together have allowed, if not contributed to, stagnation in fish harvester incomes, failing enterprise viability, and a more challenging labour supply outlook. The nature and extent of this underperformance and the impacts on labour force development are explored in this chapter within the wider context of Canadian fisheries.

BRITISH COLUMBIA LABOUR FORCE PROFILE

Statistics Canada tax filer data provides a clear picture of the age profile of people reporting taxable income from fishing employment. In 2016, the average age of fish harvesters in British Columbia was 47.4 years. The average in the Canadian industry overall was 46.7, with only Newfoundland and Labrador having an older harvesting workforce than British Columbia among coastal provinces at 48.7. Figure 9.1 compares the age profile of British Columbia fish harvesters with other provinces and the Canadian industry overall.

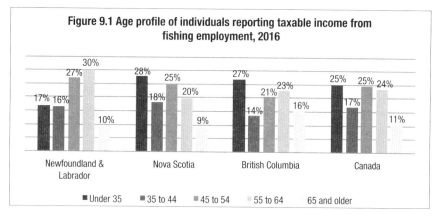

Figure 9.1 Age profile of individuals reporting taxable income from fishing employment, 2016

This tax filer information confirms that British Columbia and Newfoundland and Labrador have relatively older fish harvesting labour forces, with close to two-fifths of harvesters approaching or above retirement age (65) in the industry. More positively, British Columbia has a larger proportion of harvesters in the younger cohort (<35 years) than some other provinces, perhaps reflecting recent increases in new entrants from Indigenous communities. However, the relatively greater representation of harvesters still working past the age of 65 years is striking. Of concern as well is the relatively small proportion of British Columbia harvesters (14%) in the 35–44 age group, including future owner-operators and many people with young families in fishing communities.

As explained in previous chapters, the 2015 CCPFH survey of fish harvesters did not generate robust findings for British Columbia harvesters because of sample size limitations. However, some findings from a 2004 CCPFH survey, conducted with a much larger sample population, are still relevant.[71] Table 9.1 shows findings from the survey of captains.

TABLE 9.1 CCPFH 2004 SURVEY OF FISHING CAPTAINS, ATLANTIC PROVINCES AND QUEBEC, AND BRITISH COLUMBIA

	Atlantic & Quebec (N=1,205)	British Columbia (N=300)
Average age	48	56
% planning to retire within 10 years	34%	44%
% having some difficulty recruiting and retaining crew	20%	53%
Reasons for problems in recruiting and retaining crew		
Wages too low	50%	55%
Seasonal nature—not enough weeks of work	26%	46%
Fewer young new entrants	10%	22%
Advice to young person considering a career in fisheries		
Strongly discourage	23%	48%
Slightly discourage	19%	18%
Slightly encourage	34%	28%
Strongly encourage	24%	6%

These survey responses suggest that more than a decade ago British Columbia captains were older than their eastern Canadian counterparts and faced greater challenges attracting and retaining new labour supply in terms of available people, incomes, and career prospects.

The 2004 CCPFH survey also generated some still-pertinent findings from questions directed at crew workers, shown in table 9.2.

TABLE 9.2 CCPFH 2004 SURVEY OF FISHING CREW, ATLANTIC PROVINCES AND QUEBEC, AND BRITISH COLUMBIA, RESPONSES ABOUT FUTURE EMPLOYMENT PLANS		
	Atlantic and Quebec (N=900)	British Columbia (N=171)
I plan to continue as crew member	56%	66%
I plan to buy enterprise, become captain	40%	13%
I plan to leave fishery, move to a non-fishing job	4%	17%

Although the crew sample population was somewhat younger in British Columbia, they reported more years working in the industry and lower expectations of becoming enterprise heads.

The 2004 survey results for both captains and crew do not describe an industry with positive prospects. We are today seeing the downstream consequences of serious human resources challenges identified fifteen years previously.

As figure 9.2 illustrates, British Columbia stands out from all provinces except Manitoba with regard to the participation of Indigenous people in the commercial fishery. Canada Census information confirms that in 2016 nearly one thousand Indigenous individuals reported being employed in fishing, representing nearly a quarter of the total fishing labour force in British Columbia. Indigenous communities have long provided significant proportions of the labour force in Manitoba and British Columbia, while in eastern Canada Indigenous participation began to rebuild after the Supreme Court's *Marshall Decision* in 1999 opened up access to fishing rights and resources. Key

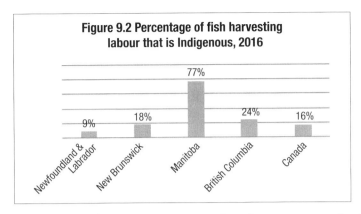

Figure 9.2 Percentage of fish harvesting labour that is Indigenous, 2016

informants in British Columbia assert that there are now far fewer Indigenous participants in the commercial fishery than there were in the 1990s.

FISH HARVESTER EMPLOYMENT AND INCOMES IN BRITISH COLUMBIA

Statistics Canada tax filer data indicates that the total number of individuals reporting taxable income from fish harvesting employment in British Columbia declined by 21%, from 7,191 to 5,675 over the 2000–2016 period. The decline was not as pronounced as in Newfoundland and Labrador (-47%) but much steeper than in Nova Scotia and New Brunswick (both -4%).

In terms of fish harvesting incomes, table 9.3 compares changes for Canada and five provinces in average fishing employment incomes in constant dollars (2016) over the 2000–2016 period.

Year	NL	NS	NB	Que	BC	Canada
TABLE 9.3 CHANGES IN AVERAGE PRE-TAX FISHING EMPLOYMENT INCOME, 2000–2016 (CONSTANT 2016 $)						
2000	$19,343	$28,359	$19,133	$21,205	$20,677	$20,950
2009	$12,961	$19,062	$13,122	$14,480	$16,606	$14,561
2016	$27,002	$40,434	$33,992	$30,161	$20,640	$30,449
Change 2000–2016	40%	43%	78%	42%	0%	45%
Change 2009–2016	108%	112%	159%	108%	24%	109%

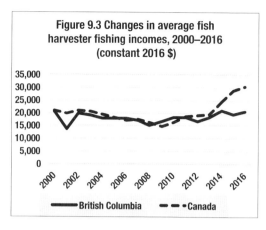

Figure 9.3 Changes in average fish harvester fishing incomes, 2000–2016 (constant 2016 $)

British Columbia harvesters started out the period with incomes close to the Canadian average and held that position through the early 2000s. Since 2009, they have fallen behind relative to harvesters in other provinces, and in 2016 had after-tax, after-inflation incomes equivalent to earnings in 2000. As evident in figure 9.3, after 2009, the bottom year for the fisheries downturn, incomes for all harvesters rebounded but at a slower rate in British Columbia than elsewhere.

In terms of employment and earnings outside primary fish harvesting jobs, the tax filer data suggest that British Columbia fishermen participate in OP at about the national average rate (29.1% in British Columbia compared to 30.6% nationally), but their average earnings at $24,470 in 2016 were significantly higher than for Canadian harvesters overall ($20,903). Curiously, average OP incomes increased substantially over the 2000–2016 period (+33%) for Canadian harvesters overall, but there was only marginal improvement in British Columbia (+5%).

TRENDS IN THE FISHING ECONOMY

Two sets of metrics are useful in measuring performance in the fishing economy: the value of fish landings (i.e., gross revenues fish harvesters receive from sales of fish) and value of exports. The latter is critical because roughly 90% of Canadian fish landings are destined for export.

TABLE 9.4 CHANGES IN LANDED VALUES, 2000–2017 (CONSTANT 2017 $, MILLIONS)

Year	Atlantic Provinces and Quebec	British Columbia
2000	$2,433	$507
2009	$1,633	$305
2017	$3,399	$398
Change 2000–2017	+ 40%	- 21%
Change 2009–2017	+ 108%	+ 30%

Table 9.4, drawn from DFO's statistical services, illustrates the sharp contrast in trends for value of landings in constant dollars (2017) in British Columbia compared to Atlantic Canada and Quebec.[72] All regions saw a sharp decline during the 2007–2008 recession, and all have recovered since 2009. However, the fall in British Columbia was much steeper and the recovery weaker. While the fisheries are evidently contributing more to incomes and local economies in eastern Canada, this data suggests that gross revenues in after-inflation dollars flowing into fishing enterprises and fisheries-dependent communities in British Columbia are significantly lower in 2016 than they were in 2000.

With regard to exports, the federal Department of Innovation, Science and Economic Development (ISED) provides up-to-date information on the value of exports by province and product group on its interactive website.[73] Figure 9.4 shows the value of exported seafood products ("Fish, Crustaceans, Molluscs and Other Aquatic Invertebrates") in constant dollars (2017), comparing 2009 with 2017 for British Columbia and Atlantic Canada. The value of British Columbia seafood exports grew over this time period by 31%, compared to an 81% increase in the Atlantic provinces. This information confirms the growth in global demand for seafood products and British Columbia's apparently lagging performance, but it is somewhat misleading in that it includes output from aquaculture producers (e.g., fish farms, cultured shellfish). While aquaculture generates a relatively small proportion of Atlantic Canadian exports, farmed salmon alone contribute more than half the value of British Columbia seafood exports.

The ISED statistical resource on exports also provides data by industry as defined by North American Industry Classification System (NAICS) codes. Figure 9.5 shows the value of exports from 2009 to 2017 for the "saltwater" fishing industry.[74] These values are lower than in figure 9.4 because they cover mainly live and minimally processed seafood products (e.g., live lobster, whole fresh fish) and do not include many value-added processed products or aquaculture products. Nevertheless, the trends are consistent with those in table 9.4: the value of seafood exports is growing at a lower rate in British Columbia (17%) than in the Atlantic provinces (92%).

Defenders of the fisheries status quo in British Columbia often attribute the more significant growth in the east coast fishing economy to the lobster fishery alone. But, as discussed in chapter 2, in Atlantic Canada the rising market tide seems to be lifting all boats. The British Columbia industry is also seeing improved landed value per tonne, though not to the same extent as on the east coast. There is strong growth in shellfish revenues but only limited gains in groundfish and pelagics in British Columbia.

There is of course a different species mix in Pacific fisheries, but industry structure also plays a role. Landed value reflects prices paid at the landing site and not necessarily the final value in the marketplace.

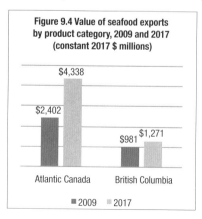

Figure 9.4 Value of seafood exports by product category, 2009 and 2017 (constant 2017 $ millions)

$4,338
$2,402
$981 $1,271

Atlantic Canada   British Columbia

■ 2009 ■ 2017

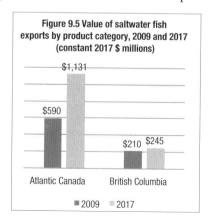

Figure 9.5 Value of saltwater fish exports by product category, 2009 and 2017 (constant 2017 $ millions)

$1,131
$590
$210 $245

Atlantic Canada   British Columbia

■ 2009 ■ 2017

The people who actually fish on the water may receive only a limited portion of the real market value of what they produce, depending on who owns the licence or quota they are fishing. As well, vertical integration—that is, fisheries firms being free to operate at all levels in the value chain from harvesting through to processing and marketing—gives companies in British Columbia much greater leverage to suppress the price of fish to the harvesters and to transfer profit-taking to higher levels in the value chain.

The total value of fish landings and exports is of course impacted by the volume of fish brought to the market as well as by final product prices in the market. It is therefore important to assess the extent to which the economic impacts of different fisheries are a reflection of market-driven fluctuations in product prices as distinct from ups and downs in the volume of production. Using DFO statistics, figure 9.6 shows year-over-year changes in landed volumes and landed value in the British Columbia fishery from 2000 to 2015, indexed to the year 2000.[75]

Figure 9.6 reveals that significant increases in landed volumes in the 2000–2004 period in British Columbia did not drive up total landed values, and that the rebound in values after 2012 was not primarily a result of increased landings.

Figure 9.7 provides data for the same relationship for fisheries in the Atlantic provinces. Landed values closely tracked volume of

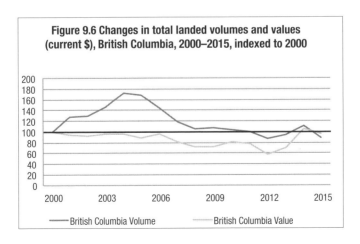

Figure 9.6 Changes in total landed volumes and values (current $), British Columbia, 2000–2015, indexed to 2000

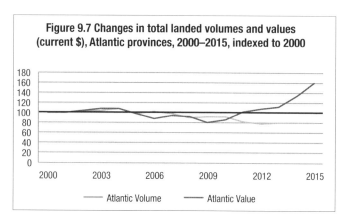

Figure 9.7 Changes in total landed volumes and values (current $), Atlantic provinces, 2000–2015, indexed to 2000

landings until 2009, after which values surged upwards through 2015 while landings remained flat.

Finally, figure 9.8 makes the same comparison for Alaska fisheries which are particularly pertinent because the species mix is similar to that of British Columbia.[76]

It would appear that Alaska fisheries have experienced consistent and substantial growth in landed values over the period, supported by modest growth in landings. The 80% improvement in landed values substantially outpaces the Atlantic provinces fisheries (at 60%), suggesting that the Atlantic lobster fishery is not the only difference maker between the overall economic impacts of Atlantic and Pacific fisheries.

These comparisons raise a very basic and challenging question as to why the British Columbia fishery is not seeing the growth in

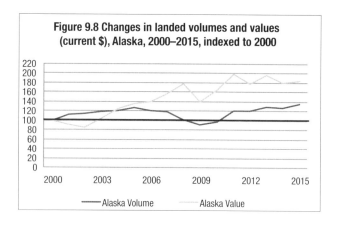

Figure 9.8 Changes in landed volumes and values (current $), Alaska, 2000–2015, indexed to 2000

product values that are evident in other regions. The evidence suggests the need for a deeper look at the structure of the British Columbia industry and at current linkages between British Columbia fisheries and global seafood markets.

RELEVANT STUDIES

Two in-depth studies address the economic performance and unique labour supply challenges facing the fishing industry in British Columbia but do so from different perspectives.

In 2013, the BC Seafood Alliance published a report on labour supply challenges in the fish harvesting sector, drafted by fisheries economist Gordon Gislason.[77] The report explores what it describes as the "daunting challenges" facing the British Columbia fishing industry in terms of "an aging workforce that is difficult to retain, emerging certification and skill requirements set by regulation, and barriers to the intergenerational transfer of fishing assets and the entry of young people to the vocation."[78]

The report focuses on the unique aspects of the harvester workforce, including the prevalence of informal recruitment and training processes; a relatively older age profile of employees compared to the wider working population in British Columbia; and the significant proportion of Indigenous and visible minority participants. The report also makes note of seasonality issues and the reliance of fish harvesters on non-fishing income. "Due to the short seasonal nature of many fisheries, fishermen can also work outside the industry in activities such as construction, house repair and sport fish guiding. Federal government tax filer data indicates that in 2006 the average fisherman earned $33,700 of which 57% or $19,100 came from fishing."[79]

Gislason identifies a number of critical labour force recruitment and retention issues, including high rates of turnover in crew and low crew wages, particularly in salmon fleets, and lack of access to capital for new entrants to become owner-operators.[80] The report links these recruitment and retention challenges to the more basic problem of faltering enterprise viability in British Columbia's fishing fleets.

> Most crew recruitment and retention problems are rooted in the economics of the fishery—if fleets were more profitable and wages were higher, and the industry provided more stable predictable employment, many human resource issues would abate e.g., less turnover, more crew willing to undergo training.[81]

The report identifies significant differences in the role of EI in the British Columbia fishery compared to Atlantic Canada, resulting largely from a lack of industry input into local EI policies and practices in British Columbia.

> B.C. fishermen report extreme difficulty in accessing EI funds and receiving training at the same time. In contrast, it appears that Atlantic Canada fishermen have much less difficulty doing so. Our discussions with Atlantic Canada fisheries organizations suggest that, while the EI regulations are consistent across Canada, the interpretation of the regulations can vary regionally even by different federal offices within the same province.[82]

Gislason confirms the potential value of training and other supports to facilitate OP options.

> The industry and its workforce need to adapt to the changing business conditions and to be more flexible in its future practices. The fishing workforce needs to increase its education level and to reskill not only to meet mandatory certification requirements but also to meet this flexibility challenge. One component of this reskilling may be to meet the needs of not only the fishing industry of the future but also a variety of other occupations on water or on land.[83]

To overcome these labour force challenges, Gislason concludes that major structural and policy changes are needed to improve enterprise viability and career prospects in the industry.

> *The industry faces daunting labour recruitment and retention problems, problems inextricably linked to the economic fortunes of the industry....*
>
> *The youth of today are looking for vocations that not only fit their lifestyle and aspirations but also pay well and can provide long-term, stable employment. The businessman [sic] of today is looking to invest in businesses which are stable, economically prosperous and for which financial institutions will provide loan capital. Many segments of the B.C. fishery fail these tests. And this failure, in some cases, is tied to fisheries management practices.[84]*

Another substantial research report, carried out by Ecotrust Canada and the T. Buck Suzuki Foundation in 2014, takes a different view on the kinds of fisheries management policy changes needed to support labour force renewal. They make the case that, in the absence of Owner-Operator and Fleet Separation Policies, the introduction of catch shares or individual transferable quotas (ITQs) that trade in more or less open markets has marginalized many fishing enterprises and made it increasingly difficult to attract and retain new labour supply.

> *What we learned is that the commercial fishery has experienced a fundamental restructuring—not just a simple reduction in size and strength. Access to local resources is moving into fewer and fewer hands. Attempts to make fisheries safer, more cost-effective, and more secure for fishermen have not, by all accounts, achieved their goals....*
>
> *Our research has shown that catch shares without clear social objectives, and specifically B.C.'s ITQ system, have had deleterious effects across the board. The system has made fishing more expensive, more complicated, and less safe. It has resulted in higher unemployment both in the industry and in broader economies, made ex-fishermen wealthier than active fishermen, reduced the number of new entrants into this sector,*

and limited the financial viability of future generations of fishermen. We would argue that catch shares have essentially privatized a public resource and radically reduced the ability of smaller vessels and communities to benefit from the industry.[85]

The report provides a case study of an independent inshore fishing enterprise that fishes an average halibut quota of 7,740 pounds to earn $54,180 in gross revenue. The vessel also catches the average amount of salmon (23,785 pounds) for a trolling licence. If the enterprise owned the halibut quota outright, it would gross $109,500 from both fisheries. Of this amount, after operating costs, maintenance, and insurance, the boat and two-person crew would share $62,000 in income over a few months of fishing.

However, if—as is more and more often the case—the enterprise has to lease the halibut quota, the crew share is sharply reduced. At current rates (at the time of the study), leasing the halibut quota would cost $38,700, meaning that the lease owner would be pocketing 71% of the landed value while taking none of the risks involved in actually fishing the quota. Since operating costs, maintenance, and insurance are fixed costs, the direct effect would be to reduce the boat and crew share from $62,000 down to about $34,000. The report states,

> *Leasing places a major burden on crews and skippers, turning fishermen into sharecroppers on their own boats. And it can carry additional financial risk: many fish companies lease their quota to fishermen under the condition that the fishermen sell them any fish they catch—at prices set by the company. This turns fishermen into 'price takers,' removing their ability to negotiate prices or take advantage of market spikes....*
>
> *Catch shares claim to improve fishermen's finances by allowing them to take advantage of good timing, getting higher prices when they land fish in periods of high consumer demand. But any advantages are cancelled out by the stress of high lease prices, ever-thinning margins, and loss of agency around establishing relationships with buyers.*[86]

The catch share report concludes by posing the question of whether a different fisheries management framework might lead to renewal of the fishing economy and rebuilding of the labour force in British Columbia.

The growth of catch share management systems has contributed both directly and indirectly to the decline in commercial fishing activity on the B.C. coast. The introduction of access rights was intended to support independent fishermen. Instead, it has consolidated access away from fishermen, led to new quota costs, increased financial risk for small-boat fleets, and given rise to armchair leasing by wealthy individuals, seafood processors, and retailers. B.C.'s commercial fisheries land more than $300 million annually. How might we manage and monitor this industry to get a different set of results—jobs, viable coastal seafood industries, resilient communities, and a new generation of fishermen producing our food? And should we have basic social objectives when we impose private property rights on a public resource?[87]

The Gislason and Ecotrust Canada reports come at these issues from different starting points, but in their final analyses they agree on one fundamental issue: renewing the fisheries labour force in British Columbia must begin with rebuilding business viability for fishing enterprises. The fishery in British Columbia, as elsewhere, will attract new labour supply if and when it can pay competitive wages, provide secure jobs, and promise rewarding careers. The challenge is to identify innovative policy approaches, management models, and export development strategies to generate these better outcomes.

A BETTER FUTURE FOR BRITISH COLUMBIA FISHERIES?

The evidence reviewed in previous chapters supports the overall view that the fishing industry in Canada holds potential to drive significant economic growth in regions and communities that need it, but that looming labour shortages are a threat to the realization of this potential. The evidence surveyed in this chapter suggests that the labour force challenge may be even greater in British Columbia because the industry's weak economic performance will seriously counteract any efforts to attract and retain new entrants.

The British Columbia fishery appears to be more driven by volume of landings than by market demand and rising product values. In a policy environment centred on ecosystem-based sustainability of marine resources, efforts to grow the industry should instead pursue continuous improvements in product values and in access to local, regional, and global markets. Relative to comparable jurisdictions, the British Columbia industry does not appear to be pursuing this course.

A big part of the challenge in British Columbia is that industry stakeholders are deeply divided on the causes of the apparent stagnation. Spokespersons for companies, quota owners, and other defenders of the status quo attribute all the blame to the decline of salmon fisheries over the last thirty years, insisting that the industry is too complex to restructure and that such efforts risk more harm than good. "It's too late to unscramble the omelette," they argue.

Leaders in harvester organizations challenge these views, pointing out that it is in no one's interest that the industry is unable to sustain its labour force. They have proposed practical solutions to regulate exorbitant leasing costs and to strengthen owner-operator fleets so that fishing communities, including First Nations communities, derive greater benefits from adjacent resources.

In June 2019, the federal government passed Bill C-68 to revise the Fisheries Act. Along with restoring habitat protections and recognizing Indigenous rights, a major goal of C-68 was to entrench in legislation two policies long in effect only for inshore fisheries in Atlantic Canada and Quebec: Fleet Separation (fish companies can't own fishing licences or quota) and Owner-Operator (only the owner can fish a licence or quota). During hearings on C-68 in the House of Commons Standing Committee on Fisheries and Oceans (SCOFO) a flood of industry stakeholders from British Columbia provided compelling evidence of dysfunction and fundamental unfairness in DFO licensing policy in the Pacific region. They challenged the committee to consider why there was no commitment within Bill C-68 to improve the social and economic benefits generated by fisheries in British Columbia.

In response to these pressures, the committee launched a special study on DFO policy in the Pacific region. Their report, titled *West Coast Fisheries: Sharing Risks and Benefits*, endorsed by all committee members from the three major parties, described the current state of the British Columbia fishery as unsustainable and urged the DFO minister to set in motion a process to build a more equitable licensing regime. The following excerpt from the report's conclusion provides a fitting close to this chapter.

> *The committee believes that the West Coast commercial fisheries fall short, and lag the east coast's and some of the world's fisheries, in how they benefit active fishers and their coastal communities. In the opinion of the committee, the vitality of a fishery should be examined by looking at its economic and community benefits as well as its ecological health.*
>
> *As the status quo is not economically and socially sustainable, the committee calls on DFO to facilitate, foster and implement grassroots initiatives for change within each fishery that have gained the support from most of that fishery's participants. The committee is convinced that a successful transition toward a more equitable quota licencing [sic] regime must be "made-in-British Columbia" and supported by all participants, including vessel/licence owners, active fish harvesters, processors, and First Nation[s] and non-First Nation[s] coastal communities.[88]*

This conclusion drawn by the SCOFO policy review is entirely consistent with the findings and policy advice generated by the CCPFH FLMI study.

Chapter 10

BUILDING A FUTURE

The labour market challenges facing the fish harvesting industry in Canada are complex and far-reaching. To meet them will require strategies that are equal in scale, intensity, and scope. "Strategy" in this context means an integrated, longer-term initiative to plan, coordinate, and oversee efforts by leaders and lead organizations in industry, government, and fisheries-dependent communities.

The highest priority, strongly advocated by industry stakeholders, is to pursue policy, program, and regulatory changes to *enhance the viability of fishing enterprises*. The goal is to build more economically resilient fishing fleets that can themselves draw in new labour supply with higher incomes, stable employment, and attractive career prospects. Most economists agree that labour shortages ultimately result from weaknesses on the demand side rather than of lack of supply, even if the new supply needs to come from outside the communities that employers traditionally draw upon.

However, on the supply side, industry leaders and harvesters at the community level also understand and support the need for new initiatives to *facilitate new entrant recruitment and intergenerational transfer of fishing assets*. Realistic opportunities to become enterprise owner-operators in a growth industry will, over the medium term, be critical for retaining the younger cohort within the current labour force and for attracting ambitious and committed new entrants. Expanding the supply of young harvesters and equipping them to become owner-operators will also facilitate transition for the many enterprise heads now reaching retirement age.

The third strategic direction—*to facilitate occupational pluralism*—presents unique challenges. Periods of seasonal unemployment make fishing a less attractive career choice in many areas, so having ready access to rewarding jobs in non-fishing seasons could help overcome this constraint. However, industry leaders are justifiably concerned that expanded OP could jeopardize employee retention and reverse years of progress toward fish harvester professionalization. With looming labour shortages in many other occupations, however, rural development leaders believe that, with local leadership and careful planning, OP could contribute to rebuilding the available labour supply for fisheries and other rural industries.

(CCPFH)

This final chapter surveys these three elements of a comprehensive strategy to rebuild and renew the fish harvesting labour force in Canada.

ENHANCING FISHING ENTERPRISE VIABILITY

Review of developments in the industry, in Canada and elsewhere, and consultations with industry stakeholders have helped to identify ways to improve enterprise viability in Canadian fishing fleets. Two core directions are proposed: changes in fleet structures, licensing policies, and fisheries management plans to lengthen seasons and diversify fishing activities; and harvester participation in industry-wide initiatives to improve market demand and product values.

DEVELOPMENT OF MULTI-SPECIES ENTERPRISES AND LONGER FISHING SEASONS

Before the introduction of limited entry licensing and the establishment of Canada's 200-mile exclusive economic zone in 1977, a fishing licence was a simple permit or registration that allowed harvesters to participate in many different fishing activities. Over the course of the year, harvesters might be active in shellfish, groundfish, and pelagic fisheries, hunting seals, and perhaps shoreline harvesting of clams, mussels, and seaweeds. They could also choose which gear to use, from anchored nets and traps, to jigging, longlining and trolling, mobile bottom trawl, and midwater seine nets.

Limited entry licensing transformed the single open permit into a portfolio of licences for individual species, often restricted by gear type and fishing zone. The 1980s saw the development of larger and faster vessels going greater distances, with electronic navigation and fish finding and more productive fishing gear. In response, the primary goal of fisheries management policy became the protection of fish stocks in a context of significant harvesting and processing overcapacity—"too many fishermen and not enough fish." In the 1990s, collapses in groundfish and pelagic stocks in Atlantic Canada and dramatic ups and downs in salmon catches in the Pacific region, resulted in the reduction by half or more of inshore fleets in Newfoundland and Labrador and in British Columbia.

By 2000, the great majority of fishing enterprises in Atlantic Canada were specialized in one or perhaps two harvesting sectors. Lobster remains the dominant fishery for inshore vessels in the Maritimes, while crab and cod are the leading species in Newfoundland and Labrador. The snow crab, scallops, shrimp, herring, and haddock fisheries each have small fleets of specialized midshore or offshore vessels. While some inshore vessels have licences and quotas for crab, halibut, large pelagics, etc., the majority of enterprises generate their revenues from one species. As a result, many millions of dollars are tied up in progressively more productive and more expensive vessels that in most cases are mainly active in only one fishery over a few months of the year.

In short, while fisheries management plans and licensing policies in Atlantic Canada have been effective in mitigating the overcapacity problem and achieving sustainable harvesting levels, the overall result is fleet structures and fishing operations that are inefficient. With limited seasonal operations, both fixed capital (vessels and gear) and labour are underutilized in most fleets. In recent years, there has been substantial investment by both government and industry in rationalizing fleets and consolidating fishing enterprises, but limited attention has been given to the possibility of evolving to multi-species fleets operating over longer seasons.

Current trends in Atlantic fisheries may make such a transition more feasible as a policy objective over the next decade. After the region-wide groundfish collapse in the 1990s and severely curtailed catches, groundfish stocks are gradually rebuilding—most notably the northern cod stock in Newfoundland and Labrador, but also halibut and red fish stocks in the Gulf of St. Lawrence, halibut on the Scotian Shelf, and haddock on Georges Bank. As well, improved profitability for fishing enterprises in key sectors is providing more owner-operators with investment capital and incentives to innovate with their licence portfolios, business models, and harvesting activities.

The accelerating retirements of older harvesters together with limited numbers of new entrants will create more opportunities and perhaps greater pressure to consolidate fishing enterprises within inshore fleets in ways consistent with new Owner-Operator and Fleet Separation regulations under the revised Fisheries Act. And with rising licence, quota, and enterprise prices, and higher crew wages, owner-operators may see more incentives to innovate their business models to manage higher operational costs and start-up debt loads.

Given these demographic and economic factors, the industry in Atlantic Canada, within vigorously enforced Owner-Operator and Fleet Separation regulations, could evolve in some regions to smaller fleets of better capitalized and more diversified inshore enterprises. There are indications of such a shift with the greater involvement of inshore vessels: in the snow crab fishery in the southern Gulf and the Scotian Shelf, expanding lobster catches in southern Newfoundland, and the expanding halibut fishery. There is anecdotal evidence of more problematic changes. For example, enterprise owners in some areas are finding ways to accumulate licences in more than one lobster fishing area to fish more than one season.

A highly pertinent example of this new direction in Atlantic Canada's fishing industry is the work now being done in Newfoundland and Labrador to prepare for the return of large-scale codfish harvesting. The 2017 fishery for northern cod landed approximately 13,000 metric tonnes, but DFO fisheries managers now anticipate that the total allowable catch (TAC) may double or triple over the next decade. A CBC News story explains how the industry is preparing to manage this growth potential.

Last April [2017], a group of processors and representatives from the Fish, Food and Allied Workers Union formed the Newfoundland and Labrador Groundfish Industry Development Council. The council is also looking toward a quality-based cod fishery with a longer season that could compete with Iceland....

Last year, the council submitted a proposal to the federal Department of Fisheries and Oceans to restructure catch allowances for cod off eastern Newfoundland. Instead of opening the fishery to different vessels for small periods of time throughout the season, it proposed weekly catch limits. With the new limits, nearly 10,000 tonnes of cod came out of the water, more than double the catch from the year before. This year, the council asked that the weekly limits go up and the season be extended.[89]

Before the 1994 moratorium, inshore cod was a glut fishery with the majority of the TAC being landed during warm summer weeks and processed into lower-value cod blocks and salt fish. Recognizing that demand for such products has virtually disappeared, and needing to rebuild enterprise revenues to offset declining crab and shrimp landings, the Fish, Food and Allied Workers Union (FFAW-Unifor) has been partnering with progressive processing interests to plan and implement a transition to high-quality fresh and fresh frozen codfish products for export to higher value markets. The union has negotiated quality standards and a price structure that rewards quality and is providing training to harvesters in proper handling and transport of fish from the water to the plant.

The FFAW-Unifor is also working with processors and DFO fish managers to implement weekly catch limits to reduce gluts and spread codfish landings over a longer season. The goal is to encourage harvesters to organize their fishing activities to take advantage of the accessibility of different species at different times of the year. Union leaders foresee a time when many inshore enterprises could be active for eight to nine months of the year fishing different combinations of cod, halibut, lobster, crab, shrimp, mackerel, herring, capelin, lumpfish, seals, and other species depending on what is available in local areas.

Another important example in Newfoundland and Labrador is the management of the expanding halibut fishery in the Gulf. Rather than introduce an ITQ regime[90] that would have given a few enterprises control of the entire quota, perhaps creating another small specialized fleet, a management plan was developed to distribute the quota among a larger number of inshore enterprises to complement fishing activities in shellfish, other groundfish, and pelagics and thereby improve overall fleet viability.

In the Maritimes and Quebec, where up to 90% of inshore enterprises participate in the lobster fishery, there is, at present, less diversity in fishing operations. In the Southern Gulf and on the Scotian Shelf, some harvesters are active in snow crab, tuna, and halibut fisheries along with lobster. With higher catches and prices for lobster and crab, producing bait has also become a lucrative sideline for some enterprises that target mackerel, herring, and other pelagics.

In British Columbia, most fishing enterprises are multi-species operations. Traditionally, salmon has been the anchor fishery, the great majority of harvesters having area licenses in troll, seine or gillnet fisheries for salmon. However, with declines in some key salmon stocks and sharp ups and downs from year to year, they also need to fish for halibut, sable fish, crab, shrimp, herring, geoduck, rockfish or other species. To sustain their enterprises many harvesters lease quota and licenses in diverse fisheries, and high leasing costs often offset the advantages of multi-species operations in terms of net revenues.

With examination of currently operating models in Canadian and international fisheries and from consultations with industry stakeholders it becomes clear that there are workable options to diversify fishing opportunities and lengthen fishing seasons to improve enterprise viability.

There are already examples and precedents for ministerial decisions to transfer licenses and fishing quota from specialized fleets to multi-species fleets through government supported buyouts or industry-based market transactions. Key examples are a snow crab allocation to the Maritime Fishermen's Union, recent transfers to First Nations, allocations of shrimp to harvester organizations in the Maritimes, or groups of inshore harvesters pooling capital to purchase quota from specialist fleets to share among members.

In situations where growth in stock abundance allows new allocations or expanded TACs, the government has the option to prioritize multi-license enterprises rather than specialized fleets. This has recently happened in the Newfoundland halibut fishery, with recovery of northern cod stocks and the management plan for Scotian Shelf snow crab.

There are many possible innovations in license and quota ownership structures including combining of enterprises, family enterprises, partnerships, professional corporations and harvesting co-operatives. Working examples include "buddying up" or combining in Newfoundland and Labrador and elsewhere. There are interesting examples in the Shetland Islands and elsewhere of co-ops set up to own and operate fishing enterprises while retaining ownership and control of licences and quotas within fishing communities.

There could also be greater flexibility in setting fishing seasons so harvesting enterprises are better able to allocate fishing effort among different species at times of peak abundance and market demand. The New England lobster fishery, for example, operates year-round except during spawning periods.

Trip limits or weekly landing quotas also encourage enterprises to spread out harvesting activities and landings over longer seasons, as is now the practice in the Newfoundland and Labrador cod and halibut fisheries.

In British Columbia and the United States there are working models for licence and quota banks where groups of fish harvesters purchase fishing rights to lease to members and new entrants at manageable cost levels. The Pacific Coast Fishing Conservation Company is an interesting model in British Columbia.

And in Newfoundland and Labrador the fisheries research centre at Memorial University is working on the development and testing of new vessel prototypes that can accommodate a variety of fishing activities and utilize more productive harvesting equipment with fewer crew workers. Such vessels would adapt new technologies like automated baiting machines for longline fishing and automated fish jigging equipment.

Which if any of these approaches will work in any particular fishery, fleet, or region will depend on the available fishing opportunities and seasons as well as local port markets, processor and buyer interests, the capacities and priorities of harvester organizations, access to project funding and investment capital, and a variety of other existential factors. Like any complex change process, the development and implementation of strategies to diversify fishing operations, restructure fleets and enterprises, and innovate with seasonal fishing operations will involve risks and uncertainties and will therefore require an extended timeframe and intensive consultation and stakeholder engagement from the outset.

There clearly are many possible avenues to pursue to build more viable fishing fleets with capacities to attract and retain the needed new labour supply. The most critical challenge at this time is that there is no lead agency for the fishing industry overall that is positioned, resourced, and mandated to bring industry, government, and community stakeholders together to develop and implement workable strategies.

HARVESTER-PROCESSOR COLLABORATION TO BUILD PRODUCT VALUE

As has been emphasized in other chapters of this report, the recent surge in revenues to fishing enterprises and export earnings for Canadian seafood products is largely the result of market-driven growth in product values rather than greater production volumes. The evidence is clear that continuing improvements in harvester incomes and future growth in the fishing economy overall will depend on industry capacities to deliver high-quality products to high demand markets.

A recent report by Gardner Pinfold Consultants, produced for Agriculture and Agri-Food Canada's Seafood Value Chain Roundtable, identifies significant potential to add value to Canadian seafood products.[91]

> *Canada's seafood industry (capture fisheries and aquaculture) fails to extract maximum value from the resource. Using a case study approach involving eight species, the minimum amount by which actual value falls short of potential is estimated in this report at about $440 million, based on 2015 and 2016 production and prices....Assuming the same factors were at work for the industry as a whole, the loss of potential value would amount to about $600 million (about 10% of Canada's seafood exports of $6.3 billion in 2016).[92]*

In key fisheries such as lobster, snow crab, and haddock, the report identifies ways to add value or to improve efficiency. Regarding the lobster industry:

> *Lobster is Canada's highest value fishery resource. From a marketing perspective, the industry has adapted well to rising volumes, shifting market conditions, and volatile exchange rates; yet output value could be higher:*

> * *Industry does not fully utilize the raw material, producing a substantial waste stream that could offer by-product potential with an estimated minimum value of $45 million.*
> * *Poor early season quality in some LFAs [Lobster Fishing Areas] results in a loss of value that could be addressed by taking steps to slow landings or adjusting seasons (admittedly an extreme measure).*
> * *At an estimated 8–10% lobster mortality is excessive; cutting it to 2% could yield upwards of $140 million in additional export revenue.[93]*

The Gardner Pinfold report suggests that the haddock fishery could build value by improving at-sea harvesting practices:

> *Haddock is one of Canada's highest value finfish species....Nonetheless, there are steps the industry could take to increase output value: Producing*

a higher quality product begins with improved at-sea handling. This mean making mandatory the adoption of what are standard practices in fisheries elsewhere: bleeding, gutting and icing fish at sea. This would require a phase-in period to allow vessel modifications, and an adjustment of the gut-loss ratio to eliminate this disincentive to adopting best practices.[94]

By way of contrast, the Gardner Pinfold study found the Newfoundland and Labrador codfish industry to be optimizing market potential and production efficiency at current harvesting levels:

Quality is a factor explaining Canada's relatively strong price performance. In contrast with the Nova Scotia haddock fishery, bleeding and gutting at sea is mandatory on NL vessels, regardless of size and gear type. This results in higher quality raw material and longer shelf life. Whether the NL industry can maintain this level of quality as the northern cod fishery recovers and TACs increase is the key challenge. This would require the harvesting and processing sectors to scale up capacity substantially, if TACs increase to 10–20 times the current level.[95]

Part of the success of the Newfoundland and Labrador industry stems from the relatively high level of organization on the harvesting side.

The NL fishing industry is highly organized, featuring a strong union representing the interests of both harvesters and plant workers. The union influences various aspects of the structure and operations of the fishery including the related matters of setting minimum fish prices and establishing quality standards through a dockside grading system. Unlike other provinces in Atlantic Canada, the price system ties price levels to defined grade standards and criteria (e.g., colour, texture, bruising).[96]

After conducting in-depth case studies of seven marine fisheries and farmed salmon, the Gardner Pinfold study concludes that the critical factor in achieving higher product values is a shift away from "volume-driven decision-making" toward a "market-driven model."

Implicit in the market-driven model is the high level of coordination between harvesting and processing that provides industry with greater ability to respond to price signals concerning what products to produce, in what quantities, when, and for whom. Few of the fisheries reviewed in this report demonstrate this level of coordination. Without it, the Atlantic inshore fisheries will remain volume-driven and value maximization will remain an elusive objective.[97]

The Gardner Pinfold report identifies "key initiatives" to meet this challenge to achieve higher product values including

mandatory quality standards in all fisheries; researching and implementing by-product opportunities; reducing mortality; promoting greater coordination between the harvesting and processing sectors, either through permitting more extensive integration in the inshore fisheries or working towards a greater level of coordination between the sectors that achieves the same result, namely, greater control over the value chain; and developing a Canadian seafood brand.[98]

The above quotation touches on the fault line in current efforts to achieve the greater coordination between the harvesting and processing sectors. The continuing attempts by some industry sectors to achieve "more extensive integration" (i.e., vertical integration) has undermined the efforts of others to develop collaborative cross-sectoral approaches. Collaboration is built on mutual respect, good faith negotiation, and recognition of contrasting interests, while the push for vertical integration involves one sector attempting to take control of fishing licences and quota away from another.

Community case studies carried out during the CCPFH FLMI study illustrate the challenges involved in pursuing industry coordination. The Newfoundland and Labrador cod fishery has been successful in building product values in large part because there is an established structure in place—union representation and collective bargaining—through which harvesters and processors are able to work together to pursue a shared goal for industry growth.

In contrast, industry-wide co-operation in the lobster fishery in the Maritimes is less evident because of fragmented industry organization and frequent conflicts over access rights. While there has been progress on issues like MSC certification, in most areas there are no well-established institutional vehicles for continuing cross-sector collaboration. The refusal of harvesters and processors in Nova Scotia to accept a one-cent-per-pound levy to support lobster marketing is a dramatic case in point, as described in this *CBC News* report: "A 'unanimous no' vote this week has put the future of a Maritime-wide lobster marketing levy in doubt. The levy would take one cent per pound from fishermen and another cent per pound from buyers to pay for a generic marketing campaign run by the industry. In Nova Scotia, the levy would raise $1.8 million annually from fishermen."[99]

In key informant interviews, processing sector stakeholders described past efforts to introduce quality grades and pricing to the lobster industry. Harvesters are reluctant to make the needed investments in selective harvesting and improved handling and storage without guaranteed price premiums. Some processors reported having tried grading standards and price incentives, only to find that rival buyers were paying top price for all lobster, independent of quality level. In a situation of intense competition for resource supply to plants, the more responsible processors were losing out and the experiments came to an end.

Industry collaboration to improve product values is not just a question of attitudes or behavioural change: the key factor is industry organization. As noted above, the expanding cod fishery in Newfoundland and Labrador is meeting with success because of an established system of contract negotiation enshrined in provincial legislation. But for lobster in the Maritimes, neither the processors nor most harvesters operate within organizational structures with capacities and mandates to negotiate binding contractual agreements or to pursue industry-wide value chain collaboration.

There is nothing particular about lobster fishing that requires this lack of structure. Prince Edward Island, for instance, has an industry-wide strategy for lobster marketing, and the industry in the state of Maine makes substantial investments in marketing with joint funding from a levy system.

> *The Maine Lobster Marketing Collaborative (MLMC), founded in 2013, is funded by Maine Lobster harvesters, dealers and processors to grow demand, both for whole live lobster and a variety of value-added products. The MLMC supports that objective by promoting the core values of the Maine Lobster industry, which are sustainability and traceability that's deeply rooted in tradition. Maine Lobster achieved the Marine Stewardship Council (MSC) certification in 2013, allowing Maine Lobster to certify its long-standing sustainable practices. The industry has been self-regulating for more than 150 years.[100]*

In Australia there is an impressive history of harvesters and processing interests working together to pursue mutual interests through a lobster supply chain management strategy called the "Clean Green Program." The program, industry-developed and owned, covers vessel safety management systems, on-board occupational health and safety, food safety, and quality handling practices, animal welfare, and environmental and sustainability management.[101]

And there is some history of concerted efforts in Canada to advance such industry co-operation. In 2007, DFO partnered with the CCPFH on a national "From Ocean to Plate" consultation process, with regional stakeholder conferences and a national roundtable. The latter event was attended by representatives of fish harvester organizations from seven provinces, processing sector leaders, and officials from provincial governments and two federal departments. The objective for the roundtable was "to provide a forum for industry, Fisheries and Oceans Canada and provincial governments to identify skills and learning activities that can be initiated by the CCPFH and its industry and training sector partners to address the From Ocean to Plate agenda and shared objectives for improved fleet viability."[102]

The DFO director general for resource management set out the overall objective for DFO's "From Ocean to Plate" initiative as being "to coordinate policies and programs relevant to fish harvesting, aquaculture, processing, distribution and marketing to maximize economic value." To achieve this objective, DFO committed to lead a comprehensive national strategy, developed through broad-based consultations, encompassing initiatives in eco-labelling, fleet restructuring and integrated fisheries management planning.

The proceedings report from the roundtable identified broad areas of consensus on moving forward with "From Ocean to Plate" initiatives. There was overall agreement in principle with the goals. Key objectives shared among DFO, the provinces, harvester organizations, and other partners were identified as fleet restructuring and rationalization where needed, enhanced enterprise and community viability, and improved product quality and value. The national roundtable also found consensus on action priorities for industry-government collaboration, including:

- *Development of a branding and marketing strategy centred on telling our story as professional owner-operator fish harvesters based in coastal communities, and as stewards of marine resources*
- *Promotion of product quality and enhanced product value*
- *Promotion of stewardship and responsible fish harvesting practices*
- *Development of options and capacities for fleet restructuring*
- *Development of options and capacities for fisheries co-management and "co-science."[103]*

The "From Ocean to Plate" process demonstrated the willingness of harvester leaders to take seriously the need for concerted action to improve product quality and to assure access to international markets through eco-labelling, traceability, and responsible fishing initiatives. It laid important foundations for future industry efforts to achieve MSC certification for key fisheries and for fleet restructuring programs in several provinces.

A key to the success of "From Ocean to Plate" was the participation of senior officials from DFO and the provinces throughout the planning and consultations. Harvester participants felt they were part of a process that could have real impacts on policy and program decision-making. The significant failing was that processing sector representatives did not participate on any scale and were not part of the emerging strategies and action priorities.

As directed by its board comprised of fish harvester leaders, the CCPFH has continued to support value-chain collaborations, including recent efforts with member organizations and processing companies to develop training components to support quality improvement and marketing for Newfoundland and Labrador northern cod, Prince Edward Island oysters, and New Brunswick snow crab.

In summary, under the right circumstances, fish harvester leaders and their organizations are willing and able to address the challenges identified in the Gardner Pinfold report to build and sustain product value within a Fleet Separation/Owner-Operator Policy environment. The evidence reviewed here would suggest that attention needs to focus on the interface between the harvesting and processing sectors.

With the Owner-Operator and Fleet Separation policies now supported in legislation and regulations, vertical integration will remain limited in the most valuable fisheries in the Atlantic region and Quebec. In this environment, efforts to grow the economic value of fisheries will require a focus on new structures and capacities for harvester-processor collaboration. In addition to the five Gardner Pinfold action priorities for building product value, a sixth priority might be added: legislative and regulatory mechanisms to create legitimate processor and harvester organizations where they don't already exist, with responsibilities and mandates to negotiate contractual agreements binding on all members. Without such a change in industry structure it is doubtful that any of the other priorities will be easily achieved.

FACILITATING RECRUITMENT AND INTERGENERATIONAL TRANSFERS

Evidence presented in earlier chapters identifies the likelihood that up to 40% of current owner-operators of fishing enterprises in Canada will have retired out of the industry by 2025. There are a number of significant policy challenges arising from this prospect. In a 2017 survey of owner-operators in the Maritimes on intergenerational transfer issues, written-in comments by two respondents highlight some of the key issues.

> *I inherited my father's licence and I do not owe a cent on my fishing enterprise and I would never borrow. If I had to sell, I would ask $900,000 because everything is new and at 50,000 to 60,000 pounds of lobster at $8 a pound I make $450,000 so why would I sell? Never! In three years, I'm a millionaire.*[104]

> *Our fathers—our predecessors, the fishermen before us—fought to preserve their independence and by the same token, ours. This independence has been greatly reflected in our community. Today, fishing enterprises are viable, so contribute much more to the vitality of coastal regions. If fishermen who want to retire cannot find buyers, because the money is not available, two questions arise: After working so hard to build them up, will fishermen not receive what their enterprises are worth? In the future, won't big companies or corporations want to get their hands on these valuable fishing licences? In both cases, we can only expect a loss in the economic potential of coastal regions, which will have repercussions beyond the limits of our communities. My solution would be to give a guarantee to lenders to increase the accessibility of money for new entrants.*[105]

A sharp decline in younger entrants to the industry over the past twenty years means that, in many fisheries, the number of crew workers in a position to become enterprise heads is insufficient to sustain current fleet structures. And because of the long-term pattern of low fishing incomes, many current crew workers who aspire to become enterprise heads may not have sufficient savings and/or borrowing capacity to purchase enterprises at fair market value.

In terms of access to capital, processors have long provided loans to new owner-operators in return for resource supplies to their plants, and harvester organizations accept this. However, faced with greatly increased costs of licences and enterprises, processor-lenders are looking for greater security for such loans, which is partly why some made use of controlling agreements. An unintended consequence of more rigorous enforcement of the Owner-Operator and Fleet Separation policies may be reduced access to this source of loan financing for new entrant harvesters.

As more fish harvesters reach retirement age there is a growing risk of greater division among harvesters and within their organizations. Some may turn against Owner-Operator and Fleet Separation policies in Atlantic Canada if they see them as limiting their "right" to sell for fair market value or, more simply, to the highest bidder. And in British Columbia, the absence of these policies raises the possibility that more and more licences and quota could fall under the control of non-harvesters whose business objectives are rental income and speculation on future resale value. As well as impacting resource stewardship, such a scenario could make it increasingly difficult to recruit and retain new enterprise heads and crew workers.

As discussed, given the long-standing uncertainty in Atlantic Canada about the Owner-Operator and Fleet Separation policies, harvester organizations have been reluctant to pursue licensing options and other innovations to facilitate intergenerational transfers. With the new Fisheries Act (Bill C-68) and regulations bringing greater policy stability, there may be more openness in future to new approaches on how fishing rights are owned and transferred and how new entrant harvesters gain access to investment capital. The following discussion of ways to facilitate labour supply renewal and intergenerational transfer is premised on the expectation of this more stable policy environment.

GENERAL RECRUITMENT CHALLENGES

The challenge of insufficient crew workers positioned to take over from retiring owner-operators is a consequence of the long-term decline in recruitment to the industry workforce overall. The lack of new entrants to the fishery is itself a symptom of the wider demographic and population mobility trends in rural regions. There are only three possible sources of new labour supply to any rural industry: natural population growth (more births than deaths) in rural coastal regions, domestic labour mobility (interprovincial or urban/rural), and international migration. The evidence is convincing that all three of these sources have been trending negatively in most fisheries-dependent regions for some time. The exceptions include regions with high levels of engagement in fisheries by Indigenous communities (e.g., Manitoba).

It is also a fair assumption that shortages of crew workers and rising wages will spur greater investment in replacing labour with more productive vessels and automated fishing gear. The research findings suggest, however, that special efforts will still be needed—perhaps even more so—to attract and retain sufficient workers with the more advanced skills that would be needed in more technologically advanced fishing operations. Therefore, any broad strategy to facilitate intergenerational transition in the fishery will need to take account of the more basic need to rebuild the total workforce. In consultations during the CCPFH FLMI study, industry experts and stakeholders, identified a number of policy and program options.

IMMIGRATION

In the Pacific region there is a long history of international immigrants finding success in the fish harvesting industry from places as far away as Japan, Vietnam, and eastern and northern Europe. This is not the case in eastern Canada in the fishery and other rural industries, but in recent years business and community leaders have made special efforts to change this pattern. In Nova Scotia, the ONE Nova Scotia Commission produced an influential report (the "Ivany Report") challenging rural communities to open their doors to new immigrants, and a change in attitudes is increasingly apparent in that province. Prince Edward Island has also had success in drawing in international immigrants to start businesses and stabilize communities.

Restrictions on the use of temporary foreign workers in the fish processing sector throughout eastern Canada have sparked growing interest in permanent immigrants. Federal and provincial collaboration on the Atlantic Immigration Pilot, "designed to help Atlantic businesses of all sizes attract international graduates and skilled foreign workers to fill job vacancies" has created a vehicle to accelerate access to new employees from overseas.[106] The opportunity is there for harvester organizations to mobilize their members to access new labour supply through the program to meet current and future needs.

RECRUITMENT AND CAREERS PROMOTION

The greatest challenge to attracting new labour supply to fish harvesting is the widespread view that the fishery is in decline and offers few opportunities. While many fish harvesters themselves are more optimistic about the future, the news may not be reaching the wider world. There were frequent mentions in community and industry consultations that guidance programs at the high school and community college levels provide little or no information on career opportunities in fish harvesting, even in fishing regions. Stakeholders felt that for too long parents and school authorities have been counselling young people to move away from their communities and rural industries, and these attitudes need to change.

Systematic provision of information to young people in high school and community colleges on employment opportunities, income levels, and the lifestyle attributes of fishing careers could help stem the outflow of young people from fishing communities. There are isolated examples of successful programs where students are doing work placements on fishing vessels, completing mandatory safety training and gain credits toward the Fishing Master IV qualification while in high school.

Industry and community leaders in other countries have recognized the need to rebuild the fishing labour force and they are pursuing a variety of innovative strategies to achieve that goal. A recent report from the University of Alaska describes such approaches, including youth permits, or student licences, and mentorship and apprenticeship programs to allow new entrants "to gain experience, learn fishing skills, and/or earn fishing income without the financial burden and risks of purchasing market-based access rights."[107]

In Maine, the Eastern Maine Skippers Program provides students and prospective fishermen with training and mentorship to become successful in the industry. The training covers fisheries governance, business planning, communications, and maritime safety. "The program strives to produce graduates who are prepared to become flexible, skilled and knowledgeable commercial fishermen who have attained leadership skills and industry expertise in order to serve as advocates for their fisheries and communities."[108]

Industry and community groups in Maine have developed the Lobster Limited Entry and Apprentice Program to protect access for young people growing up in fishing communities.[109] To become a "lobsterman" through the program, a person must complete 200 days or 1,000 hours of at-sea fishing time over a minimum of two years. The state also issues special licences to youth still in school to draw them into the industry. "To qualify for a student license, an individual must be a full-time student…between the ages of 8 and 22. Students can fish up to 150 traps and must log 1,000 hours onboard by their 18th birthday (or 22nd if attending college). If students complete the program prior to their 18th or 22nd birthday, their entry into the zone is not dependent on retiring trap tags (like non-student apprentices)."[110]

From 2001 to 2011, 847 new lobster licences were issued in Maine and roughly half were issued to students.

In Norway there is a recruitment quota for young harvesters to acquire fishing rights at no cost. Eighty-four young fishermen in Norway received recruitment quota between 2010 and 2016, and only two subsequently left the industry, while several others went on to develop fishing businesses with more vessels and more quota.[111]

After the United Nations Human Rights Committee declared that the Icelandic ITQ system violated the human right to work, a coastal fishing program was created by the Icelandic government in 2009. The program allows residents of coastal communities in four regions to use up to four jig machines to harvest up to 650 kg of groundfish per day, four days per week, May through August, without purchasing ITQs. Some 750 boats participate in this fishery nationwide. This provides opportunities for young people to get started in the industry and to build up capital to purchase quotas.[112]

Iceland also introduced a Community Quota in 2003 through which community members are given free shares of quota to be landed in their home port. This program is small—less than 2% of the total cod catch—but it provides an opportunity for young people to get started in the industry. Another interesting innovation is that Icelandic fishing communities maintain the right of first refusal on the sale of fishing enterprises to buyers outside the community. Through local government or non-profit organizations, communities can buy, own, and resell enterprises, all at market rates.[113]

Denmark provides another interesting example of ways to get new entrants started in the fishery.

Denmark has launched a new subsidy scheme to help young fishermen buy their first vessel, in a bid to help a 'generation shift' in Danish fisheries. The 'growth and development package for Danish fisheries' has allocated DKK 10 million [$2M Cdn] to the subsidy scheme to help fishermen under 40 gain a foothold in Danish fishing.…Fishermen under 40 can apply to take part in the first-time pool, managed by the fisheries fund.… Support is granted up to 25% of the purchase price for a new vessel, but with a ceiling of DKK 500,000 [$105K Cdn].[114]

And finally, as an example of a significant policy commitment on a national level, a bipartisan bill currently making good progress through the US Congress proposes to create a national program to encourage new entrants to fisheries.

> *The Young Fishermen's Development Act was introduced in the U.S. House of Representatives and Senate this spring [2017], and sponsoring legislators hope the bill will help break down the barriers young fishermen face. The bill is modeled after the U.S. Department of Agriculture's successful Beginning Farmer and Rancher Development Program, which launched in 2008 and is credited with preparing hundreds of young people for agricultural careers.…Using the farmer's program as a template, coalition members designed a bill that would work for fishermen.[115]*

The main elements of the act are as follows:

- *Competitive grant program for collaborative state, tribal, local or regionally based networks or partnerships*
- *Mentorship/apprenticeship program to connect retiring fishermen and vessel owners with new and beginning fishermen*
- *Support for regional training and education programs focused on sustainable and accountable fishing practices, marine stewardship and sound business practices*
- *Grants may not exceed a period of longer than three years, with a maximum grant amount of $200,000/year*
- *$2 million annual authorization for six years for program implementation.[116]*

These examples from other countries confirm two points: serious demographic and labour supply challenges are not unique to the Canadian fishing industry, and extraordinary measures and creative innovations are needed to address them. The most frequent options would appear to be:

- Training programs and at-sea experience for school- and college-age youth
- Formal apprenticeship and mentoring programs
- Free or low-cost access to start-up licences and quota for new entrants
- Community or local industry ownership or control of access rights
- Grants or low-cost loans for new entrants.

ADVANCES IN FISH HARVESTER PROFESSIONALIZATION

A long-standing challenge in recruitment of new entrants to fish harvesting has been the lack of formal apprenticeship systems to provide pathways to careers and owner-operator status. Labour recruitment to the fishing industry throughout Canada has traditionally been through informal processes: young harvesters grow up working in family or community-based enterprises and learn the trade through hands-on experience and local mentorship. Only recently have any mandatory training standards been imposed across the industry through Transport Canada safety regulations, and they are still unevenly applied.

The sharp downsizing of fleets since the 1990s and general demographic trends in rural regions—falling birth rates and out-migration—have seriously interrupted traditional recruitment and training processes. Key informants in different areas described communities where a whole generation of young people has grown up without exposure to fishing work, and there are fewer captains and vessels available to provide mentorship and at-sea learning experiences. And even with diminished fleets, there simply aren't enough potential new entrants in fishing families and communities to replace retirees in the near future.

The bottom-line challenge is that the traditional informal recruitment and training processes simply cannot generate the new labour supply needed to meet looming requirements. To find the numbers required, new entrants will need to come from non-fishing backgrounds in rural communities, from adjacent urban regions, from interprovincial migration, and from international immigration. Effective apprenticeship programs will therefore be needed to provide the combination of hands-on, at-sea experiential learning and classroom-based knowledge and skills development in an efficient and almost fast-track manner.

Two provinces—Quebec and Newfoundland and Labrador—have fully operational apprenticeship systems in place. In the latter case the mandatory training and experience standards are integrated with DFO licensing standards, so participation in the program is universal. In Quebec the link to the licensing system has not been formalized and so the regime is more limited in impact. Nevertheless, in both these provinces, a new entrant coming to the industry with no prior experience in fishing would have a clear path to becoming a fully qualified crew worker and potential owner-operator within a defined time period. In no other province is such a pathway formally established. Training is available in most regions, but it is not mandatory and is not linked into experiential learning and mentorship and sea-time components.

Training and apprenticeship fall within provincial jurisdiction but linking licensing standards and the use of registration revenues to support certification regimes requires federal collaboration. DFO initiated the development of professionalization programs in the 1990s, but much work remains to be done to have fully functioning systems in place throughout Canadian fisheries.

LABOUR MARKET INFORMATION

One of the core findings from the CCPFH survey of fish harvesters and from community case studies is that there is insufficient information to inform current harvesters and potential recruits about diverse employment opportunities in fish harvesting and also in non-fishing occupations outside fishing seasons.

In terms of opportunities within the fishing industry, in Newfoundland and Labrador, the Professional Fish Harvesters

Certification Board has a well-used website informing harvesters about employment opportunities on fishing vessels. This helps captains find crew and crew workers find jobs across different fishing seasons. In the Maritimes there is a growing informal network of harvesters, including captains, who fish one lobster season in their home areas and then crew on vessels in other areas during different seasons. Flexibility in the EI system to allow double claims provides incentives for this form of OP, but expanded and better targeted LMI services could better facilitate such mobility and make employment in the industry more attractive with longer seasons and higher incomes.

The larger concern regarding LMI is outreach to potential new entrants beyond the immediate catchment areas. As mentioned above, stakeholders identified the need for more information on fishing careers to be available in public schools and community colleges. It was also clear from consultations that fishing employers are not familiar with, and do not make wide use of, Service Canada's job listing systems and other LMI tools at the provincial level. It will also be the case that opportunities in fisheries are not communicated through international immigration recruitment programs, and much work may need to be done to develop industry capacities to use these resources.

One possible recruitment strategy in the Atlantic region particularly would be to target the many thousands of people who grew up in fishing communities, and were perhaps once employed in fishing work, and who left their home regions to go to Ontario and western Canada in the 1990s and 2000s. An interview with a former Regional Director General from DFO Gulf region revealed that licensing rules in that region were recently adjusted to allow individuals to regain their "core" licence holder status despite having worked away for more than the previous limit of two years. The explicit intent of this flexibility was to help overcome growing labour shortages and to encourage individuals who had accumulated savings while working away to get back into the industry and become owner-operators.

In Newfoundland and Labrador the Professional Fish Harvesters Certification Board is receiving growing numbers of applications from individuals who left fishing to work away and now want to return and regain their status. Some applicants have continuing employment in other industries or regions but want to be able to come back to fish full-time during certain seasons. While these individuals represent a needed source of new labour supply and are potential purchasers of enterprises from retirees, they also raise concerns about the possible undermining of professionalization standards and a return to the days of "moonlighter" harvesters who take fishing rights and resources away from committed professionals. The certification board is examining options to manage these risks and opportunities.

The important takeaway from these examples is that there may be potential to draw back people who left when the industry was at a low point. Those who might now return will, possibly with savings to invest, because the industry is rebuilding. The challenge will be to develop LMI tools to identify and communicate with such individuals through family and community networks and other means. Consideration might also be given to providing financial incentives to offset the costs of relocation and restarting in the industry, as is done in other countries as well as in other industries in Canada.

However, the more important longer-term challenge will be to link up LMI tools and resources with career guidance programs in schools and colleges and with immigration services. It will also be important to familiarize employers and employees in the fish harvesting industry with the available online tools and other LMI resources for both recruitment and job search. The use of LMI tools to support harvester engagement in appropriate forms of OP outside fisheries will be discussed below.

ACCESS TO AFFORDABLE CREDIT

Financial supports for new entrants to the fishing industry are uneven and fragmented across Canada. Nova Scotia and New Brunswick both have dedicated fisheries loan agencies, although in the latter case the board is being merged within an integrated fisheries, aquaculture, and agriculture board. In both provinces recent policy changes now allow loans for purchases of licences as well as vessels and gear, and there are incentives for new entrants with more generous interest rates and loan conditions. However, these agencies account for only a small proportion of the lending that goes on in the industry. With a $9.5M budget, the New Brunswick board makes less than a dozen loans per year. The Nova Scotia Fisheries and Aquaculture Loan Board operates with a $6.4 M budget and currently holds loans for about $110M. These services would have to be scaled up substantially if they are to begin to meet current levels of need.

In Prince Edward Island loans to fish harvesters are managed through the regular small business loans agency. Newfoundland and Labrador provides a loan guarantee program. Neither of these provinces offers targeted supports or incentives for new entrants. British Columbia has no specialized fisheries loans program.

A significant shift in harvester access to credit came with the DFO decision in 2008, as part of the PIIFCAF Policy, to allow licences as well as fixed capital to be used as collateral for loans from "recognized financial institutions." The bulk of financial transactions involving licences has since shifted to commercial institutions.

A recent survey of new owner-operators in New Brunswick and Nova Scotia found that half had received loans from banks and credit unions.[117] The remainder had inherited their enterprises or had borrowed from family members or fish processors. When asked why they had not borrowed from provincial fisheries loan boards, the respondents indicated that they either were unaware of the boards' services or considered them to be remote, slow, and bureaucratic. Bank and credit union lenders were described as being locally accessible and having expertise in the fishing business.

The CCPFH national sector study report in 2005 anticipated the intergenerational transfer challenge and identified policy and program options to address it.[118] These included expanded loan board services, tax measures, and collective ownership models. In particular, the 2005 report discussed options for the federal government to play a role in providing more consistent and supportive access to credit in the fisheries sector modelled on the extensive financial support system in the agriculture industry.

Agriculture and Agri-Food Canada has focused significant policy attention on demographic and labour supply challenges in the farm industry that parallel those in the fishery. Intensive industry consultations to develop the Next Agricultural Policy Framework generated the following outlook for federal government leadership on human resources issues.

> *Access to qualified labour is a major issue for the sector....The [Next Agricultural Policy Framework] is an opportunity to focus on addressing labour shortages by attracting and retaining skilled workers....The strategy should focus on improving the public image of agriculture as a viable career choice amongst youth, educating youth on the wide range of opportunities in the field, and providing programming that caters specifically to youth and women....*
>
> *According to the 2011 Census of Agriculture, the median age of farm operators was 54. With the coming wave of retirements, a stronger focus on farm transition and new entrants is suggested. Investing in training and skills development, succession planning, farm transition and overall business planning would help enable knowledge transfer and the migration of producer operations from those seeking to retire to the next generation of farmers. Given the health of the sector and developments in agricultural technology, it was suggested that now is a great time to generate enthusiasm and interest in agriculture careers through engaging youth and encouraging new entrants.[119]*

The Canadian Agricultural Loans Act program provides farmers with access to loans of up to $500,000 for purchasing land and constructing or improving buildings, and up to $3 million for agricultural co-operatives. These loans are administered through local financial institutions and involve low interest rates and down payments with flexible repayment options. The program also provides more generous supports for new entrant farmers.[120]

**FARM CREDIT CANADA—
YOUNG FARMERS**

FCC creates products and services
that meet the unique needs of the next
generation of farmers. Customized
financing through the Young Farmer
Loan, under-40 events, plus tools
and advice help take your business
to the next level. We're here for your
journey—every step of the way.
If you're a qualified producer under
40, the Young Farmer Loan can
help you take the next step in your
agriculture career.
Features
⊗ Purchase ag-related assets up to
  $1,000,000
⊗ Closed variable rates at prime plus
  0.5%
⊗ No loan processing fees
⊗ Special fixed rates available
⊗ We finance
⊗ Lines of credit
⊗ Crop inputs
⊗ Livestock
⊗ Equipment financing
⊗ Lease equipment
⊗ Environmental solutions
⊗ Farm transfers

See fcc-fac.ca/en/we-finance/primary-
producers/young-farmers.html

The federal government also operates Farm Credit Canada, a financially self-sustaining Crown corporation with one hundred offices across rural Canada and a $33 billion portfolio. In addition to loans, Farm Credit Canada runs financial education programs, provides financial management software tools, and promotes youth engagement in agriculture at the community level. The sidebar on this page provides details on the Young Farmers program and the resources it offers.

There are no parallel national agencies to develop and lead such strategies in the fishing industry. Given the seriousness of the labour shortages and intergenerational transfer challenges, consideration might be given to federal initiatives to partner with provincially administered agencies—in provinces that have them—to expand access to credit. Provisions could also be made for private and non-profit lending agencies to collaborate within a national framework. The mandate of such an agency could be exclusively focused on intergenerational transfer of enterprises within owner-operator fleets.

As another support for intergenerational transfers, the 2005 CCPFH report discussed the option for fish harvesters to receive the same capital gains exemption as owner-operators in the agriculture industry, and that change has since happened. However, given the sharp rise in licence prices, the exemption could be more generous than it currently is in specific situations, such as a transfer from a professional owner-operator to a qualified new entrant harvester who has served a formal apprenticeship with the seller of the enterprise. Such exemptions could require oversight by the Canada Revenue Agency in consultation with DFO licensing authorities to ensure that the benefits accrue to buyers and not sellers of licences, and that the sale of the licence is consistent with the Owner-Operator and Fleet Separation regulatory framework.

INNOVATIONS IN LICENCE OWNERSHIP STRUCTURES

During the early implementation of the PIIFCAF Policy, in-depth consideration was given to allowing fishing enterprises to incorporate for tax advantages and other purposes. An intensive consultation process, led by DFO, examined the following options:

- Wholly Owned Corporation: the simplest and most conventional model available to small businesses.
- Family-Owned Corporation: the licence holder/owner-operator would own 100% of voting shares, but family members would own some non-voting shares. This option could help to transfer the licence within the family while providing an income to the retiring harvester.
- Professional Corporation: qualified professionals can establish joint ownership of an enterprise in which they are both owner-operators and both are present during fishing operations. It is simply a way for two or more harvesters to pool capital to buy an enterprise.
- Partnership: much like the professional corporation option but not incorporated. The owners would not get the same tax advantages, but 100% of the shares would be legally and beneficially owned by two or more fish harvesters (existing licence holders or qualified new entrants) all of whom would become owner-operators and would have to be on-board the vessel during fishing operations.

⊗ Co-operative: owner-operators would establish a co-operative under appropriate legislation and collectively own and operate one or more fishing enterprises, on the assumption that the co-op members alone would fish the licences.

After two industry consultation meetings in 2008, with representatives from all major harvester organizations in the four Atlantic provinces and Quebec, a consensus emerged that these options and tools should be further refined and evaluated in greater detail. However, before accepting any option, industry representatives wanted to receive "detailed and credible information on possible risks in relation to Owner-Operator and Fleet Separation policies and access to EI," and the "potential benefits and costs analysis of each option."[121] Participants agreed that a more extended process was required, including "the convening of a working group with the right expertise and credibility to provide the information stakeholders need." The wholly owned option was clearly seen as the least risky, but industry participants wanted "all the options to remain on the table until they [had] all the information [needed] to make informed decisions."

Subsequent to these consultations, wholly owned incorporation was accepted by DFO and Canada Revenue Agency as an option for enterprise ownership, but there has been little or no follow-through on evaluation of the other options. Controversy over the effectiveness of PIIFCAF and continuing challenges to the Owner-Operator and Fleet Separation policies from within and outside government blunted the willingness of harvester organizations to consider any changes that might further undermine the independence of owner-operator fleets.[122] However, with the Owner-Operator and Fleet Separation policies in Atlantic Canada about to be entrenched in the Fisheries Act and regulations, there is a new environment in which to evaluate different options for enterprise ownership.

COLLECTIVE OWNERSHIP OPTIONS

The CCPFH 2005 report identified options for harvester organizations to take on greater roles in the disposition of licences and quotas within their fleets or communities. Where there is clearly expressed support, legitimate organizations might be given authority to purchase licences or quota to hold them out of the fishery for periods of time for conservation purposes, to lease licences and quota to new entrants as "starter licences", or to transfer them to new entrant harvesters on a long-term basis.

A 2017 policy workshop with local leaders in the Maritime Fishermen's Union (MFU) considered two options.

First, using the same approach as in the MFU's lobster licence buyback program in the early 2000s, and working through the Maritime Fishermen's Union Community of Interest local governance structure,[123] a collectivity of harvesters in a given area could buy licences from retiring harvesters using a reverse auction process, and then hold them in a licence bank to make them available to new entrants on a limited term lease, a permanent lease, or a lease-to-own basis.[124] The same could be done with snow crab quota or quota in other fisheries.

Second, regulatory changes could allow a crew member on a lobster fishing enterprise owned by a harvester approaching retirement age to purchase progressively larger blocks of traps from the owner and fish those traps on the owner's vessel until the crew member is able to take over the entire enterprise. This would provide a more gradual process for both new entrants to become owner-operators and older captains to scale down their fishing efforts and risk as they approach retirement.

While such innovations may seem out of step with current practices, there are working models that provide a basis for such innovations. In the Maritimes, for example, the MFU currently owns a quota of snow crab that is harvested by rotation among its members, with shares of profits going to support a family medical plan and community of interest initiatives, including lobster licence buyback projects. The Gulf Nova Scotia Fleet Planning Board owns quotas for shrimp and groundfish, contracts the harvesting to owner-operators, and shares profits among members. The Prince Edward Island Fishermen's

Association also has a shrimp quota, the benefits of which go to support owner-operator fleets. In DFO Maritimes region, groundfish are allocated to regional boards that administer the sharing of individual quotas. In British Columbia, a small harvester group has developed a quota bank that operates as a social enterprise to provide more affordable fishing opportunities to small-boat harvesters.

Another structural option is the co-operative. In the 1920s, fishermen's co-operatives were established in many regions to provide a means for impoverished rural communities to pool capital and build up fleet capacities and access to markets. Many of these co-ops still operate, although some function much like conventional fish-buying and processing companies rather than social enterprises. The Fogo Island Co-operative Society in Newfoundland and Labrador perhaps provides a modernized and more innovative model.

> *The Fogo Island Co-op has not only survived, it has thrived. We have reached a milestone and this year we are celebrating 50 years in business. When giants in this industry failed, the Fogo Island Co-op remained steadfast, competitive and strong.…*
>
> *The Fogo Island Co-op is a major force in the Newfoundland Seafood Industry, harvesting various species of seafood (crab, shrimp, turbot, capelin, cod, sea cucumber, herring and mackerel) in Newfoundland waters and remains an international force in markets globally. A fleet of 30 longliners, and many small inshore vessels supply quality raw material daily to three modern processing plants. The Co-op has its own laboratory, welding shop and a marine services center complete with a fishing supplies outlet.…They have developed a rock-solid reputation for honesty, integrity, pride in performance, and world-class quality.*[125]

In the Fogo Island model, individual harvesters still own all the licences and quotas. There could be opportunities to adapt the co-op structure to allow communities of harvesters to own licences and quota collectively in order to retain ownership in the community in perpetuity, all within an Owner-Operator and Fleet Separation framework.

Such a co-op would not process and market the fish, but simply manage a portfolio of licences and quotas. Exactly this model has been used in the Shetland Islands to build up midshore and offshore fleets and accumulate quota under community ownership and control.

First Nations communities have developed other models. Following the Supreme Court's *Marshall Decision*, quotas and fishing vessels are owned collectively by First Nations governments in the Maritimes and the working harvesters earn incomes based on a share of the value of the catch.[126] The Northern Native Fishing Corporation in Prince Rupert, British Columbia, was established in 1982 with $12 million funding from the federal government. The corporation took ownership of over 250 vessels and salmon gillnet licences from BC Packers company. The licences remained with the new corporation while the vessels were sold to Indigenous harvesters to establish themselves as independent owner-operators in commercial fisheries. Over its history, the corporation provided a range of supportive services to harvesters who leased licences, including training, mentoring, and access to capital. The business success of the Northern Native Fishing Corporation was blunted in later years by the decline in the salmon fishery overall, but the corporation is still in operation as a de facto licence bank.[127]

Building on these and many other initiatives in Canadian fleets and in other countries, a variety of structures and program options could be explored specifically as means to keep control of access rights in communities, to provide access to fishing opportunities for new entrants, and to make fishing licences and quotas more affordable.

OCCUPATIONAL PLURALISM STRATEGY

As discussed in earlier chapters, recent research and consultations have generated a complex picture of the role of OP in the fisheries and of the risks associated with it. On the one hand, it is a long-standing and integral aspect of how the labour market functions to provide adequate incomes in seasonal fisheries. Upwards of 30% of fish harvesters report taxable income from non-fishing employment, and this does not include income generated from self-employment and from informal economy activities. OP may also be essential in helping crew workers generate capital to become owner-operators. In the 2015 CCPFH survey, Atlantic fishing captains expressed strong agreement with the view that access to rewarding employment outside the fishing seasons could help attract and retain new entrants to the fishery labour force.

On the other hand, fish harvester organizations in most regions have worked hard to professionalize the industry, pressing for licensing and fisheries management policies that favour committed harvesters and discourage part-time or occasional participants with primary occupations outside the fishery. The objective has been to consolidate fishing access rights and income generation opportunities in the hands of people for whom fishing is a chosen career. As discussed, the highest priority for harvester leaders is to improve enterprise viability so that more harvesters generate full-year incomes in the fishery and don't have to find non-fishing employment.

Given these complexities, the goal here is to identify approaches to managing OP that enhance labour force recruitment and retention with the least risk to professionalization objectives. The CCPFH survey research and consultations identified six possible elements of a broad strategy to expand fish harvester participation in OP as a means to attract and retain new labour supply.

LMI FOR NON-FISHING EMPLOYMENT OPPORTUNITIES

In the survey findings and in community consultations, the most serious barrier to greater participation in OP was identified as lack of information about suitable jobs outside fishing seasons. As mentioned above, this applies for employment opportunities within the fishery in terms of crewing positions in other fleets and regions, as well as jobs in other industries where skills acquired in fishing could be transferable.

In both the survey and the community consultations, harvesters frequently asserted that there simply were no jobs available outside fishing seasons in their regions. However, government labour market projections and other LMI resources, as well as employers and local economic development experts, provided evidence of growing shortages in relevant sectors.

Survey respondents and industry and community key informants recommended the development of well-targeted social media tools and other networking resources to provide fish harvesters with current information about suitable employment opportunities in local labour markets. It was also suggested that these LMI programs should inform harvesters about support systems, such as training and certification services, to help them overcome obstacles.

EMPLOYMENT INSURANCE INNOVATIONS

Key informants and focus group participants described the calculations that harvesters make in considering travel to non-fishing jobs or investments to acquire skills and qualifications for employment outside the fishery. For those who qualify at the higher benefit levels, fishing EI benefits provide a secure and predictable income to carry them through non-fishing seasons. Recipients are reluctant to risk that security by taking on the costs and family disruption that come with working away. They need to be reasonably confident that the financial returns on their efforts are sufficient to justify the risk. For those without the higher levels of EI benefits, these cost-benefit calculations are all the more critical.

Carrots have perhaps been more effective than sticks in encouraging more harvesters to take these risks. Meaningful supports for the costs of job mobility and working away, and to manage family disruptions, might expand fish harvesters' participation in OP.

The research indicates that EI policies and programs are unevenly applied in different regions. The Fishing EI program requires harvesters on benefits to take on fishing jobs when they become available and Part 2 benefits are targeted on training related to fishing. However, it appears that in some regions beneficiaries on Fishing EI have been able to get financial support to train for non-fishing jobs on a seasonal basis. More work is needed to understand how the rules are applied in different regions and to evaluate the outcomes when harvesters on Fishing EI have access to training for non-fishing jobs.

For waged fish harvesters who qualify for regular EI, both the carrots and the sticks may be more sharply defined. There may be greater pressure to take available jobs outside the fishery, but also more flexible and generous Part 2 supports to prepare for such employment activities.

The CCPFH FLMI study identified compelling reasons to explore more fully the ways in which EI fishing benefits, regular benefits, and Part 2 benefits might more effectively encourage and support fish harvester participation in OP. Examination of unemployment services in other countries confirms that there are policy innovations that effectively address the wider challenges involved in rebuilding rural seasonal labour forces. Given the sensitivities around these issues, an open and collaborative approach with significant stakeholder engagement and leadership would be wise.

EDUCATION, TRAINING, AND RECOGNITION OF TRANSFERABLE SKILLS

There was clear consensus in the CCPFH surveys of both captains and crew workers that, along with targeted LMI, improved access to training for non-fishing employment would be most helpful in encouraging and facilitating greater fish harvester participation in OP. Trades occupations were identified as those most directly related to the knowledge and practical competencies involved in fishing work.

For many experienced harvesters the constraint is not an absence of competencies but rather the lack of formal certification to validate them and convince potential employers. A special study carried out as part of the FLMI study identified program options to measure and recognize knowledge and skills acquired by harvesters through on-the-job experience and suggested the use of an innovative system of "badges" as a means to communicate job competencies.

PREPARING YOUTH FOR CAREERS SPANNING MORE THAN ONE INDUSTRY/OCCUPATION

Community leaders and education and training officials were often quick to link OP to wider initiatives to address looming labour shortages across many rural industry sectors due to the same demographic and migration trends now impacting the fishery. One idea was to encourage young people in rural regions to recognize the opportunity to have rewarding lives with more than adequate incomes in their home areas if they prepare to work in more than one occupation or industry over the course of the year.

High schools and community colleges could promote this idea through guidance counselling. Colleges could offer program options to qualify in more than one trade or occupation over a two- to three-year period. For example, a college student could be part of an apprenticeship program to become a professional fish harvester while also training to be a certified electrician, bookkeeper, chef, or tourism manager. The starting point for these considerations is the recognition that all these industries will soon face labour shortages, all are more or less seasonal, and all may benefit from innovative strategies and program models to meet future labour supply challenges.

COMMUNITY LABOUR MARKET COLLABORATION

During CCPFH project consultations, community development leaders, local government officials, and economic development experts were quick to generalize from the fishing industry to identify ways in which OP might use available labour supply in rural economies more efficiently. There were references to the idea of regional industry bodies or employer councils to share labour supply on a seasonal basis.

Rather than coercive approaches, the emphasis appeared to be on sharing LMI and ensuring that unemployed workers in different sectors are fully aware of the opportunities available. There might also be collaboration in developing cross-training programs and coordinating efforts for employers to recognize the diverse competencies that workers in particular sectors develop, independently of formal training and certification systems.

ADAPTATION IN PROFESSIONALIZATION REGIMES

As discussed above, provinces that have professionalization regimes in place with apprenticeship and mandatory training standards are currently feeling pressure from inside and outside the industry with regard to labour recruitment and retention issues. Some observers have gone so far as to characterize professionalization regimes as barriers to labour supply renewal and have called for the lowering of entrance requirements and training standards.

By the same token, Transport Canada has faced stiff criticism for its new policy of requiring the Fishing Master IV qualification for all operators of fishing vessels above a certain minimum tonnage. This again is characterized by some as an unnecessary barrier to attracting new entrants to the fishery.

Another pressure on professionalization programs, and licensing standards, comes from people who left fishing years ago for careers in other industries and regions. Some are now returning and wanting to re-establish their professional status without having to start from the beginning in terms of new entrant sea-time and training. In principle, the industry welcomes such returnees and has been willing to be flexible to reintegrate this much-needed source of new labour supply and potential owner-operators. However, there are cases where the returnees are still maintaining primary careers in other industries and wish to use vacation time to make significant incomes over short periods when particular fisheries are open. Such cases are seen by harvester leaders as conflicting with the interests of committed professionals.

The findings from this study do not encourage arguments for watering down professional standards to fast-track access to fishing careers for new entrants. On the contrary, strengthening apprenticeship programs and developing professionalization regimes are seen as key long-term initiatives to promote the fishing industry as a safe and rewarding field of work. Over the medium to long term, this is the most effective means to attract new entrants who will commit to fishing as a career.

However, professionalization boards and DFO licensing officials will likely continue to face pressures from former harvesters who want to re-enter the industry. They may need to consider innovative policies and practices to support re-integration of former fish harvesters who will be committed to the industry as a primary vocation. And if fish harvester participation in OP continues to expand as it has done in the recent past, more attention will need to be given to finding ways to maintain professional standards while accepting that some harvesters will have parallel careers during non-fishing seasons. The Newfoundland and Labrador Professional Fish Harvesters Certification Board has a baseline policy that in order to maintain professional status, fishing has to be the primary source of employment income during the fishing season. This, combined with efforts to restructure fisheries management plans to have longer seasons, may provide an effective approach to managing this challenge.

LOOKING TO THE FUTURE?

The starting point for collaboration on new strategic approaches is the clear recognition of the nature and scale of the challenges involved. It is hoped that this book will provide the evidence to inform and to justify such recognition by key leaders in industry, government, and fishing communities, Indigenous and non-Indigenous. The fishing industry in Canada is at a critical juncture. Two dominant trends will transform the industry, one way or another, over the next ten years: strong and persistent growth in market demand for seafood products, and the loss through retirement of some 40% of current enterprise owners and crew workers.

The new Fisheries Act will support a shift in fisheries management objectives to take greater account of community sustainability and the preservation of the independence of harvester enterprises. If strategies and initiatives to address the labour supply challenge are planned and managed in ways consistent with this new direction, fisheries-dependent regions and Indigenous communities across Canada could experience significant economic growth, as well as social and cultural renewal. But without coordinated national and regional leadership, concerted strategies and higher levels of industry-wide collaboration, the opportunity may be lost or, at best, unevenly achieved.

Change of this nature and scale is never easy. In some regions and fleets, industry organizations are leading the way, but in others the critical capacities for planning and collaboration are not in place, and many fish harvesters are not well informed on the challenges and opportunities ahead. The risk of conflict and further industry fragmentation is high.

For these reasons, the starting point for developing new policy approaches, program tools, and collaborative strategies will need to be broad-based consultation and industry engagement with the following objectives:

⊗ Share knowledge with industry stakeholders on economic risks and opportunities, demographic challenges, and labour supply challenges

⊗ Engage with industry stakeholders at local, regional, and fleet sector levels to understand emerging challenges and to build a consensus framework on broad strategic responses

⊗ Undertake more intensive consultations and strategic planning in specific areas of change such as licensing policies, fisheries management planning, value chain collaboration, apprenticeship and professionalization, access to credit and related financial services, and management of seasonal employment diversity

⊗ Develop new regional leadership and planning capacities—involving industry, all levels of government, First Nations communities, and rural coastal communities—to facilitate cross-sector collaboration on labour force renewal and intergenerational transition.

ACKNOWLEDGEMENTS

This book draws heavily from the findings and policy analysis generated by Canadian Council of Professional Fish Harvesters (CCPFH) Fisheries Seasonality and the Allocation of Labour and Skills Labour Market Information Study. The study was funded in part by the Government of Canada's Sectoral Initiatives Program.

I am deeply grateful to the following individuals who contributed in so many ways to the research work and thinking over many years that have provided the theoretical and experiential foundations for the book:

Bill Broderick, Fish, Food and Allied Workers-UNIFOR

Doug MacDonald, DMD Economics, Nova Scotia

Earle McCurdy, former president of the CCPFH and of Fish, Food and Allied Workers-UNIFOR

Gilles Thériault, McGraw Seafood, New Brunswick

Jean Lanteigne, Fédération régionale acadienne des pêcheurs professionnels

Jim McIsaac, T. Buck Suzuki Environmental Foundation

Keith Paugh, Prince County Fishermen's Association, Prince Edward Island

Joy Thorkelson and Kim Olsen, United Fishermen and Allied Workers' Union-UNIFOR, British Columbia

Mark Dolomount, Newfoundland and Labrador Professional Fish Harvesters Certification Board

O'Neil Cloutier, Association des pêcheurs professionnels du Québec

Randy Bell, 'Namgis First Nation, British Columbia

Ronnie Heighton, Gulf Nova Scotia Fleet Planning Board

Susanna Fuller, Oceans North

Tasha Sutcliffe and Devlin Fernandes, Ecotrust Canada

The late Christian Brun, Maritime Fishermen's Union / Union des pêcheurs des maritimes

I am also deeply grateful to current and past staff of the CCPFH and project partners who made the CCPFH FLMI Study possible:

Pierre Verreault, former executive director of the CCPFH

Martin Picard, project manager, CCPFH

Michael Haan, Statistics Canada Research Data Centre, Western University

Barbara Neis, Paul Foley, and colleagues at the On the Move Partnership, Memorial University

Martha MacDonald, Saint Mary's University

Kerry Dangerfield and colleagues at Prairie Research Associates, Winnipeg

Mark Dolomount and colleagues at the Newfoundland and Labrador Professional Fish Harvesters Certification Board

I am especially grateful to John Sutcliffe who, during his time as CCPFH Executive Director, developed the original concept and objectives for the Fisheries Labour Market Information Study and oversaw the development of the funding proposal and research design.

I owe the greatest debt to the hundreds of fish harvesters and community spokespersons across Canada who participated in interviews, focus groups, and telephone surveys. Regional Fisheries and Oceans officials, provincial government officials, and independent experts also made important contributions in interviews and workshops.

I would like to thank the Donald J. Savoie Institute for the financial support to make this book possible.

Appendix 1

RESEARCH ACTIVITIES AND DATA SOURCES

The CCPFH Fisheries Labour Market Information study was initiated in 2015 with a final report made public in early 2018. The project involved comprehensive research and consultation activities, detailed below.

LITERATURE REVIEW

Relevant research and policy studies were surveyed to collate available knowledge on demographic trends, developments in the fishing economy in different regions of Canada, seasonal patterns of labour supply in fisheries-dependent communities, and social and economic factors affecting labour mobility.

ANALYSIS OF STATISTICAL AND ADMINISTRATIVE DATA RESOURCES

A variety of data resources were accessed to support analyses of fisheries labour supply-and-demand trends and demographic, income, employment diversity, and labour mobility factors. These included Canada Census, data from 2001 through 2016, Fisheries and Oceans

Canada statistical resources, Statistics Canada tax filer data, and other Statistics Canada resources.

SURVEY RESEARCH

Random sample telephone surveys of fish harvesting enterprise heads and crew members were conducted in the Atlantic provinces and Quebec, Manitoba, and British Columbia. While fish harvester organizations provided contact information for their members in some provinces, in others there was limited access to up-to-date and accurate contact information.[128] As a result, the survey findings are more statistically robust in some provinces than in others. Provincial completion rates and error rates were as follows:

2015 CCPFH FISH HARVESTER TELEPHONE SURVEY: COUNTS OF COMPLETED INTERVIEWS			
	Captains	Crew	Error Rate (19 times out of 20)
Atlantic Total	788	372	+/-2.8%
Newfoundland and Labrador	227	217	+/-4.4%
New Brunswick	233	47	+/-5.5%
Nova Scotia	201	43	+/-6.1%
Quebec	82	50	+/-8.2%
Prince Edward Island	45	15	+/-12.4%
Manitoba	95	4	N/A
British Columbia	108	35	N/A

Some key questionnaire items from a CCPFH sector study survey undertaken in 2004 were repeated in the 2015 survey to generate comparative findings on key indicators, including labour recruitment and retention issues, demographic characteristics, and enterprise viability factors.

COMMUNITY CONSULTATIONS, FOCUS GROUPS, AND KEY INFORMANT INTERVIEWS

Fieldwork was conducted in nine fishing regions across Canada to access stakeholder and key informant perspectives on fisheries labour supply, demand trends, and strategies for labour force renewal. The occurrence and impacts of OP were assessed in consultations with harvesters and their organizational leaders, with employers in local industries, and representatives of local governments, economic development agencies, and training institutions. As well, local strategies to address intergenerational transfer and labour recruitment and retention challenges, and to enhance enterprise viability, were identified and assessed.

ENGAGEMENT WITH GOVERNMENT AND INDUSTRY STAKEHOLDERS

Proactive consultations with provincial government lead agencies for fisheries development and labour force renewal were undertaken in the provinces with the most significant fishing industries. The goals were to inform policy leads and program managers about the work and to share findings and policy analyses at different stages over the life of the project.

At the federal level, presentations and consultations were also held with Fisheries and Oceans Canada (DFO) senior policy staff in Ottawa and the regions, with policy directors in Employment and Social Development Canada, and within the Employment Insurance (EI) program. There were also presentations to Agriculture and Agri-Food Canada's Seafood Value Chain Roundtable and to senior staff in the federal regional development agencies in the Atlantic region and Quebec.

On the industry and community side, over the life of the project presentations and consultation sessions were held with staff and leaders in harvester organizations, First Nations fisheries agencies, community and environmental non-governmental agencies, harvester certification boards, human resources sector councils, and at harvester workshops and conferences.

SPECIAL STUDIES

Two special sub-studies were commissioned to address issues that emerged over the life of the project.

Dr. Martha MacDonald, a labour economist at Saint Mary's University in Halifax, NS, with expertise in international employment insurance systems was engaged to analyze the influence of the Canadian EI program on fisheries labour supply and OP among fish harvesters, and to identify policy and program options within the EI system to support labour force renewal in the industry.

The Newfoundland and Labrador Professional Fish Harvesters Certification Board administers the system to register all fish harvesters in the province. With access to their harvester registration data, the board analyzed the nature and location of non-fishing employment among registered harvesters, and identified the education and training undertaken by harvesters to support their fishing activities but also their employment in non-fishing occupations.

SOURCES: FIGURES AND TABLES

Figure (a) Fisheries and Oceans Canada

Figure 2.1 Industry Canada

Figure 2.2 Industry Canada

Figure 2.3 Helgi Analytics

Table 2.1 Industry Canada

Figure 2.5 Fisheries and Oceans Canada

Table 2.2 Fisheries and Oceans Canada

Figure 2.6 Fisheries and Oceans Canada

Figure 2.7 Fisheries and Oceans Canada

Figure 3.1 Fisheries and Oceans Canada

ENDNOTES

NOTES
PREFACE

1   The Atlantic Fisheries Fund is jointly funded by the federal and provincial governments to support innovation and R&D in the fish and seafood sector. The parallel British Columbia Salmon Restoration and Innovation Fund will provide joint federal-provincial investment of $145 million to support British Columbia's fish and seafood sector. See www.dfo-mpo. gc.ca/fisheries-peches/initiatives/fish-fund-atlantic-fonds-peche/index-eng.html and www. dfo-mpo.gc.ca/fisheries-peches/initiatives/fish-fund-bc-fonds-peche-cb/index-eng.html.

2   Donald J. Savoie, *Looking for Bootstraps: Economic Development in the Maritimes* (Halifax: Nimbus Publishing, 2017), 386.

3   One qualification with this chart: the value given for exports includes aquaculture products, which were worth approximately $1 billion in 2018. The figures for landed tonnes and landed value do not include aquaculture production.

CHAPTER 1 AN EMERGING CRISIS

4   Canadian Council of Professional Fish Harvesters, Setting a New Course—Phase II Human Resources Sector Study for the Fish Harvesting industry in Canada (Ottawa, May 2005), 59. See http://www.fishharvesterspecheurs.ca/resource-centre/publications.

5   The report was released by the CCPFH in March of 2018, and is available on the Council's website. See note 1, above.

6   See www.budget.gc.ca/aceg-ccce/home-accueil-en.html.

7   Advisory Council on Economic Growth, *Unleashing the Growth Potential of Key Sectors*, Report II, 8–9, www.budget.gc.ca/aceg-ccce/pdf/key-sectors-secteurs-cles-eng.pdf.

8   Seafood exports are tracked with the product category "Fish, Crustaceans, Molluscs and Other Aquatic Invertebrates," which includes products of the aquaculture sector that contributed approximately $1 billion in exports in 2017. See www.ic.gc.ca/eic/site/tdo-dcd.nsf/eng/home.

9   Source for seafood consumption data, see www.helgilibrary.com/indicators/fish-consumption-per-capita/.

10   Caveat: approximately 80% of seafood exports from British Columbia are produced by the aquaculture industry, predominantly farmed salmon.

11   Fisheries and Oceans Canada online trade statistics for seafood products, see http://dfo-mpo.gc.ca/stats/trade-comm-eng.htm.

12   Bear in mind that the export values include aquaculture products, while the landed volume and landed values numbers are for wild-caught fish.

13   British Columbia shellfish fisheries include, in order of magnitude, shrimp, clams and quahogs, and various crab species.

14   See DFO, *Preserving the Independence of the Inshore Fleet in Canada's Atlantic Fisheries* (Ottawa: Atlantic Fisheries Policy Review, n.d.), 5, www.fishharvesterspecheurs.ca/system/files/products/Policy-PreservingIndependenceInshoreAtlanticFleet.pdf.

15   The Honourable Dominic LeBlanc, minister of Fisheries and Oceans Canada, speaking at a meeting of the Canadian Independent Fish Harvesters' Federation, Chester, NS, July 25, 2017. Minister LeBlanc's speech can be downloaded from website of the Canadian Independent Fish Harvesters Federation. See http://fed-fede.ca/publications/.

16   CCPFH, *Setting a New Course*, 25 and 33.

17   See DFO Statistics, www.dfo-mpo.gc.ca/stats/commercial/licences-permis-eng.htm. Note that Atlantic fisheries includes four Atlantic provinces and Quebec.

CHAPTER 3 ENOUGH FISH, NOT ENOUGH FISH HARVESTERS

18   Ray Bollman, Rural Canada 2013 An Update: A Statement of the Current Structure and Trends in Rural Canada, prepared for the Federation of Canadian Municipalities, January 7, 2014. See http://crrf.ca/rural-canada-2013-an-update/.

19   In 2011, there were 293 Census Divisions in Canada: 29 (10%) were CMAs, 52 were "partially-non-metro" Census Divisions (i.e., within an hour's commuting distance of a CMA), and 212 (72%) were non-metro Census Divisions. In many studies, "rural" communities are defined as Census Divisions with 1,000 or fewer inhabitants. Bollman's approach in this report has the advantage of including within the rural framework the many towns and

small cities that are remote from CMAs, are integrated with and dependent upon wider rural economies, and share many of the attributes and challenges of rural regions generally.

20 Bollman, *Rural Canada 2013: An Update*, 46.

21 Ibid., 29–30.

22 Ibid., 2.

23 In the 2016 Census the largest occupational category for fish harvesters was labelled "fishermen/women." In 2001, this same category was labelled "skippers and fishermen."

24 The total numbers in figure 3.2 include three categories of fishing occupations: "fishing masters/officers," "fishermen/women," and "fishing vessel deckhands.".

25 Employment and Social Development Canada, *Labour Mobility and Occupational Licensing in Canada*, January 26, 2017, www.cafconnection.ca/getmedia/857e3108-a923-491a-b6b5-2273ad09fb71/Employment-and-Social-Development-Canada-Labour-Mobility.pdf.aspx.

26 Roland Tusz, Erika Rodrigues, and Matthew Calver, *Interprovincial Migration in Canada: Implications for Output and Productivity Growth, 1987–2014*, CSLS Research Report 2015–19, November 2015 https://ideas.repec.org/p/sls/resrep/1519.html.

27 Ibid., 11–12.

28 Ibid., 15.

29 Ray Bollman, *Rural Demography Update 2016*, www.ruralontarioinstitute.ca/file.aspx?id=26acac18-6d6e-4fc5-8be6-c16d326305fe.

30 See *Nova Scotia Population Estimates by County, July 1, 2015* http://novascotia.ca/finance/statistics/archive_news.asp?id=11563&dg=&df=&dto=0&dti=3.

31 See Canada Census, 2001, 2006, and 2016. Data from the 2011 Census is not included because the long-form Census questionnaire was not mandatory, and data for less populated rural regions is therefore unreliable for that year. The table aggregates all such individuals who identified their primary occupation as either "Fishing master and officer," "Fisherman/woman," or "Fishing vessel deckhand."

CHAPTER 4 REBUILDING THE FISHERY LABOUR FORCE: CHALLENGES AND OPPORTUNITIES

32 Fisheries and Oceans Canada (DFO) and Transport Canada require people who work on fishing vessels—captains and crew—to be registered. However, the registration function is carried out by provincially regulated professional certification boards in Quebec and Newfoundland and Labrador, and by provincial agencies for freshwater fisheries in Ontario and the western provinces.

33 The tax filer database for the CCPFH study included any individual in Canada who received at least $1,000 in employment income from fish harvesting as reported on T1 or T4 slips and Records of Employment. The T1 file includes data from the main tax return that every individual must submit, whether or not they are self-employed. The T4 is the

employer statement issued annually to employees and does not exist for self-employed persons unless they are incorporated (and issue T4s to themselves).

34 Tax filer data for these two sub-categories of harvesters was only available up to 2015 at the time of writing.

35 Department of Fisheries and Oceans Canada online statistical services, see www.dfo-mpo.gc.ca/stats/commercial/licences-permis-eng.htm.

36 Statistics Canada, Table 11-10-0134-01 Gini coefficients of adjusted market, total and after-tax income, www.150.statcan.gc.ca/t1/tbl1/en/tv.action?pid=1110013401&request_locale=en.

37 The Honourable Dominic LeBlanc. See http://fed-fede.ca/publications/.

38 Canadian Council of Professional Fish Harvesters, *Setting a New Course – Phase II Human Resources Sector Study for the Fish Harvesting Industry in Canada*, Appendix 4.10—The Valuation Model for Fishing Enterprises, 1.

39 Canadian Council of Professional Fish Harvesters, *Setting a New Course*, Main Report, 57.

40 Ibid.

CHAPTER 5 INTERGENERATIONAL SUCCESSION AND THE STRUGGLE OVER ACCESS RIGHTS

41 House of Commons of Canada, Bill C-68, www.parl.ca/DocumentViewer/en/42-1/bill/C-68/third-reading.

42 The CCPFH survey was conducted in December of 2015. Unlike the similar CCPFH survey in 2003/04, DFO rules prevented it from providing harvester contact information, so the sample population was constructed through industry collaboration. The Newfoundland and Labrador Fish Harvesters Certification Board provided contact information for every harvester in that province, which generated the most robust sample population. CCPFH member organizations in Quebec, New Brunswick, and Nova Scotia provided lists of their members.

2015 CCPFH FISH HARVESTER TELEPHONE SURVEY: COUNTS OF COMPLETED INTERVIEWS AND ERROR RATES BY PROVINCE			
	Captains	Crew	Error Rate (19 times out of 20)
Newfoundland and Labrador	227	217	+/- 4.4%
Prince Edward Island	45	15	+/- 12.4%
Nova Scotia	201	43	+/- 6.1%
New Brunswick	233	47	+/- 5.5%
Quebec	82	50	+/- 8.2%
Atlantic Total	788	372	+/- 2.8%

43 The responses from Prince Edward Island are not provided because of the low sample size in that province.

44 To conduct its surveys, the CCPFH study was provided with harvesters' names and telephone numbers by member organizations. Except in Newfoundland and Labrador, the only way to get contact information for crew workers was to ask captain-respondents to volunteer this information, and the results were very uneven. The survey findings for crew workers therefore have limited reliability in some provinces.

45 See Ecotrust Canada and T. Buck Suzuki Environmental Foundation's reports *Just Transactions, Just Transitions: Towards Truly Sustainable Fisheries in British Columbia*, 2018, at http://ecotrust.ca/report/just-transactions-just-transitions/; and *Caught up in Catch Shares*, April 2014, http://ecotrust.ca/report/caught-up-in-catch-shares/.

46 A total of 679 captains responded to this questionnaire item. However, a number of respondents gave $0-dollar estimates, while a smaller group gave exceptionally high estimates (e.g., $20 million). To provide a conservative estimate of average perceived market value for enterprises, 107 outlier responses for less than $100K and much more than $1 million are not included in the calculation of averages shown in table 5.2. Responses from 38 Prince Edward Island captains are not shown separately because of the small sample size, but they are rolled up in the "total" category.

47 Paul Withers, "Nova Scotia Lobster Buyers Seek Compromise with Ottawa on Company Licences," *CBC News*, October 30, 2017, www.cbc.ca/news/canada/nova-scotia/lobster-buyers-fishermen-contracts-federal-government-loans-1.4376511.

48 Paul Withers, "Lobster Fisherman Defends Maligned Practice of 'Controlling Agreements,'" *CBC News*, December 20, 2017, www.cbc.ca/news/canada/nova-scotia/controlling-agreements-lobster-fishery-1.4457002.

CHAPTER 6 MEETING THE SEASONALITY CHALLENGE

49 The tax filer data on non-fishing employment income only covers waged income as reported on T4 slips issued by employers. Many harvesters may have generated income from self-employment activities outside fishing, and that would not be included in the information on non-fishing employment income.

50 Full reports from the community case studies are available on the CCPFH website, see www.fishharvesterspecheurs.ca/.

CHAPTER 7 OCCUPATIONAL PLURALISM AND THE LABOUR MARKET

51 The N represents the total number of respondents who reported having worked in non-fishing jobs over the previous year.

52 The tax filer data shown here applies only for those harvesters who reported wage income from fishing employment and excludes the larger proportion of harvesters who report income as self-employed. Industries are identified in tax filer system by NOC and NAIC codes. The information in the table is for 2013, the last year that this data was available to the CCPFH study.

53　CCPFH, *Opportunities for and Challenges of Occupational Pluralism in Seasonal Fisheries: Regional Cases from Atlantic Canada*, 30, www.fishharvesterspecheurs.ca/.

54　See COPS, "Industrial Scenario, 2017–2026: Historical and Projected Trends in Real GDP, Employment and Productivity by Aggregate Sector," http://occupations.esdc.gc.ca/sp-pc-cops/l.3bd.2t.1ilshtml@-eng.jsp?lid=14&fid=1&lang=en.

55　COPS data sets for projected employment growth by occupation and industry are available to download at https://open.canada.ca/data/en/dataset/e80851b8-de68-43bd-a85c-c72e1b3a3890.

56　See www.jobbank.gc.ca/outlookreport/location/geo0004.

57　Report on Atlantic Case Studies, 30. The *On the Move Partnership* is a multi-year national study of labour mobility across many industry sectors; see www.onthemovepartnership.ca/.

58　Report on Atlantic Case Studies, 30–31.

59　The option of "flexibility in DFO licensing policies" was only presented to captains and had to do with current limits on maintaining professional status while working away from the fishery for lengthy periods.

CHAPTER 8 EMPLOYMENT INSURANCE AND OCCUPATIONAL PLURALISM

60　Barrie McKenna, "Report on Business," *Globe and Mail*, March 18, 2016.

61　This chapter draws heavily on a detailed examination of the EI system and its current and potential links to occupational pluralism that was undertaken as part of the CCPFH FLMI study by Dr. Martha MacDonald, labour economist at Saint Mary's University in Halifax, NS. The full report can be accessed through the CCPFH website; see www.fishharvester-specheurs.ca/.

62　Total income includes income from non-fishing employment, from dividends, and other non-employment sources such as government transfer payments other than EI.

63　Employment and Social Development Canada, Employment Insurance Monitoring and Assessment Report for the 2017/18 fiscal year, last modified June 3, 2019, www.canada.ca/en/employment-social-development/programs/ei/ei-list/reports/monitoring2018/annex5.html.

64　See the CCPFH FLMI study by Dr. Martha MacDonald, CCPFH website, www.fishharvester-specheurs.ca/.

65　The amount of weekly EI benefits a claimant receives is calculated based on total insurable earnings for a required number of "best weeks," i.e., those weeks when the claimant earned the most money. In regions with the highest rates of unemployment, the calculation is based on best 14 weeks while in regions with the lowest rates of unemployment it is 22 best weeks. Once a claimant in a high unemployment region gets 14 best weeks, they have incentives to keep working longer for lower pay rates because the lower earning weeks will not bring down their benefit level. For further detail, see www.canada.ca/en/services/benefits/ei/ei-regular-benefit/benefit-amount.html.

66 OECD, *Back to Work: Canada. Improving the Re-employment Prospects of Displaced Workers* (Paris: OECD Publishing, 2015), http://dx.doi.org/10.1787/9789264233454-en.

67 The 2018 federal budget introduced further changes to EI rules to increase incentives for working while on claim and to address the needs of recipients with significant gap periods with no income between work and receipt of benefits.

68 Under the Employment Insurance Act, self-employed individuals are able to apply for EI special benefits if they are registered for access to the EI program. There are six types of EI special benefits including maternity benefits providing up to 15 weeks of income for mothers who give birth, parental benefits for a parent to care for a newborn or newly adopted child, and family caregiver benefits for claimants who must be away from work to care for a sick or injured family member. For more detail, see: https://www.canada.ca/en/employment-social-development/programs/ei/ei-list/reports/self-employed-special-benefits.html.

69 Dr. Frances Woolley, "What is EI For?," *Worthwhile Canadian Initiative* (blog), March 30, 2016, http://worthwhile.typepad.com/worthwhile_canadian_initi/2016/03/what-is-employment-insurance-for.html. Dr. Woolley is professor of economics at Carleton University and past president and conference organizer of the Canadian Economics Association.

70 Note that the average for OP employment income is derived from the population of harvesters who actually had OP jobs, and the average for EI income is only for harvesters who actually received EI. There is overlap, but they are not the exact same populations, so readers should not conclude that, on average, all fish harvesters earned X amount from OP employment and X amount from EI. In practical terms, it is likely that many of the harvesters who had OP jobs and earned average incomes in those jobs would not have applied for EI or, if they did, would have earned below-average EI income.

CHAPTER 9 UNDERPERFORMANCE IN THE BRITISH COLUMBIA FISHERY

71 CCPFH, Appendices 2 and 4, Setting a New Course.

72 See Fisheries and Oceans Canada, Seafisheries Landings, last modified January 31, 2019, www.dfo-mpo.gc.ca/stats/commercial/sea-maritimes-eng.htm.

73 Government of Canada Report: Report—Trade Data Online, Canadian total exports; see https://tinyurl.com/y3s5c2le.

74 The NAICS code for fishing states, "This industry group comprises establishments primarily engaged in the commercial catching or taking of finfish, shellfish, and other marine animals from their natural habitats." See https://bit.ly/2AHEKaZ.

75 All data in figures 9.8 and 9.9 are sourced from the DFO statistics website for sea fisheries; see www.dfo-mpo.gc.ca/stats/commercial/sea-maritimes-eng.htm.

76 Source of Alaska data, see www.st.nmfs.noaa.gov.

77 GSGislason & Associates, *The B.C. Fishing Industry—Labour Market Information*, prepared for the BC Seafood Alliance, January 2013.

78 Ibid., ii.

79 Ibid., iii.

80 Ibid., iv.

81 Ibid.

82 Ibid., 27.

83 Ibid., 31.

84 Ibid.

85 Ecotrust Canada and the T. Buck Suzuki Environmental Foundation, *Caught Up in Catch Shares*, 45.

86 Ibid., 27.

87 Ibid., 36.

88 Standing Committee on Fisheries and Oceans, Ken McDonald, Chair, *West Coast Fisheries: Sharing Risks and Benefits*, May 2019, 46.

CHAPTER 10 BUILDING A FUTURE

89 Sarah Smellie, "What If the Cod Came Back? The Push to Reinvent Newfoundland and Labrador's Fishery," CBC News, July 4, 2017, www.cbc.ca/news/canada/newfoundland-labrador/cod-comeback-feature-1.4163972.

90 Under individual quota systems, quota owners retain a right to a percentage share of the TAC. In an ITQ regime, quotas can be traded on a more or less open market. Government has often preferred ITQs as a way to rationalize fleets, allowing larger quota holders to buy out smaller enterprises. Some ITQ systems in Atlantic Canada are governed by the Owner-Operator and Fleet Separation Policies, meaning only fish harvesters can own and exchange quotas. In British Columbia quota can be bought up by processing companies and non-fishing investors, and then leased to active fish harvesters who may or may not own any quota themselves.

91 Gardner Pinfold Consultants, *Extracting Maximum Value from Canada's Fisheries and Aquaculture Resources*, submitted to Agriculture and Agri-Food Canada, September, 2017.

92 Ibid., i

93 Ibid., 38–39.

94 Ibid., 53.

95 Ibid., 62.

96 Ibid., 54.

97 Ibid., ii.

98 Ibid.

9

99 "Maritime Lobster Levy in Doubt after 'Unanimous No' by Buyers," *CBC News*, February 19, 2015, www.cbc.ca/news/canada/nova-scotia/maritime-lobster-levy-in-doubt-after-unanimous-no-by-buyers-1.2963136.

100 Maine Lobster Marketing Collaborative, "About the Collaborative," www.lobsterfrom-maine.com/about-the-collaborative/. See also Penelope Overton, "Maine Lobster Council to Keep Marketing Funding Effort Despite Critics," *Portland Press Herald*, December 14, 2017, www.pressherald.com/2017/12/14/lobster-advisory-council-votes-unanimous-ly-to-fund-marketing-collaborative/.

101 Fisheries and Aquaculture, "20th Minister's Conference to Focus on Growing Fishing Industry" (news release), January 4, 2018, https://novascotia.ca/news/release/?id=20180104001.

102 Canadian Council of Professional Fish Harvesters, *Proceedings Report—National Roundtable on the Ocean to Plate Agenda*, Montréal, September 12–13, 2007.

103 See CCPFH, *Proceedings Report*.

104 Write-in comments on a survey of members of the Maritime Fishermen's Union conducted by the author in 2017.

105 Ibid.

106 For details on the Atlantic Immigration Pilot, see www.canada.ca/en/immigration-refu-gees-citizenship/services/immigrate-canada/atlantic-immigration-pilot.html.

107 Paula Cullenberg, Rachel Donkersloot, Courtney Carothers, Jesse Coleman, and Danielle Ringer, *Turning the Tide: How Can Alaska Address the 'Graying of the Fleet' and Loss of Rural Fisheries Access?* A review of programs and policies to address access challenges in Alaska fisheries, November 2017, 4.

108 Ibid., p. 31. See also https://coastalfisheries.org/?s=eastern+maine+skippers+program.

109 See www.maine.gov/dmr/science-research/species/lobster/limitedentry.html.

110 See *Turning the Tide*, 31. See also www.maine.gov/dmr/science-research/species/lobster/documents/apprenticebrochure08-17.pdf.

111 See *Turning the Tide*, 26.

112 Ibid., 25.

113 Ibid., 26.

114 *Undercurrent News*, "Young Danish Fishermen Given Funding Pool for First Vessel," June 30, 2017, www.undercurrentnews.com/2017/06/30/young-danish-fishermen-given-funding-pool-for-first-vessel/.

115 Samuel Hill, "Generation Next: Helping Young Fishermen Join the Fishery," *National Fishermen*, July 10, 2017, www.nationalfisherman.com/national-international/generation-next-helping-young-fishermen-join-industry/.

116 Fishing Communities Coalition, "About the Young Fishermen's Development Act," n.d., http://fishingcommunitiescoalition.org/yfda/.

117 The Maritime Fishermen's Union conducted the survey in January 2018 and received responses from nineteen harvesters who had become owner-operators over the previous few years.

118 CCPFH, *Setting a New Course*.

119 Agriculture and Agri-Food Canada, "Results of Consultations on the Development of the Next Agricultural Policy Framework," last modified November 1, 2016, www.agr.gc.ca/eng/about-us/public-opinion-and-consultations/consulting-on-the-next-agricultural-pol-icy-framework/results-of-consultations-on-the-development-of-the-next-agricultural-pol-icy-framework/?id=1476470856238#summary.

120 Agriculture and Agri-Food Canada, "Canadian Agricultural Loans Act program—Helping Farmers Innovate and Expand," last modified March 3, 2017, www.agr.gc.ca/eng/programs-and-services/canadian-agricultural-loans-act-program-helping-farmers-inno-vate-and-expand/?id=1488221933411.

121 Praxis Research & Consulting, *Proceedings Report: Industry Consultations on Issuing Licenses to Corporations*, prepared for Fisheries Renewal Directorate, Department of Fisheries and Oceans, March 2008.

122 It should be noted that some harvester organizations have continued to advocate for pro-fessional incorporation as an option for fishing enterprises to link the tax advantages of incorporation with efforts to professionalize the industry and manage rising licence costs.

123 Communities of Interest are incorporated entities through which harvesters in a cluster of neighbouring ports or communities decide how to invest money from the Maritime Fishermen's Union's snow crab allocation. Communities have also implemented licence buy-back schemes and projects to seed lobster on local fishing grounds, build artificial reefs, and improve port facilities.

124 That is, put out a public offer to purchase and then choose from the lowest or most rea-sonable bids.

125 See www.fogoislandcoop.com/about-us/company-profile/.

126 Newfoundland and Labrador Fish Harvester Professionalization Board (see https://www.pfhcb.com) and Northern Native Fishing Corporation (see https://biz.bcibic.ca/northern-native-fishing-corporation).

127 Ibid.

APPENDIX 1 RESEARCH ACTIVITIES AND DATA SOURCES

128 In the 2004 CCPFH sector study, DFO provided names and contact information for every fishing licence holder in Canada. Privacy protection rules prevented DFO from providing this information in 2015.

BACKGROUND READING AND REFERENCES

1. LEGISLATION AND POLICY

Bill C-68: Statutes of Canada 2019, Chapter 14, An Act to amend the Fisheries Act and other Acts in consequence. www.parl.ca/DocumentViewer/en/42-1/bill/C-68/royal-assent.

Fisheries and Oceans Canada. *Commercial Fisheries Licensing Rules and Policies Reference Document Pacific Region*, 2019. www.pac.dfo-mpo.gc.ca/fm-gp/licence-permis/docs/commercial-licence-permis-ref/commercial-licence-permis-ref-eng.pdf.

———. *Policy for Preserving the Independence of the Inshore Fleet in Canada's Atlantic Fisheries* (PIIFCAF). www.dfo-mpo.gc.ca/reports-rapports/regs/piifcaf-policy-politique-pifpcca-eng.htm#n1.

———. *Atlantic Fisheries Policy Review—A Policy Framework for the Management of Fisheries on Canada's Atlantic Coast.* www.dfo-mpo.gc.ca/reports-rapports/regs/afpr-rppa/framework-cadre-eng.htm.

———. *Commercial Fisheries Licensing Policy for Eastern Canada – 1996.* www.dfo-mpo.gc.ca/reports-rapports/regs/licences-permis/index-eng.htm.

Gough, Joseph, *Key Issues in Atlantic Fisheries Management.* Canadian Museum of History. www.historymuseum.ca/cmc/exhibitions/hist/lifelines/gough1e.html#contents.

2. HUMAN RESOURCES AND LABOUR MARKET STUDIES

Alaska Marine Conservation Council and the University of Alaska Fairbanks. *Turning the Tide: How Can Alaska Address the 'Graying of the Fleet' and Loss of Rural Fisheries Access?* (A useful international survey of strategies for rebuilding the fish harvesting labour force.) http://fishermen.alaska.edu/turning-the-tide.

Canadian Council of Professional Fish Harvesters. *Setting a New Course: Phase II Human Resources Sector Study for the Fish Harvesting Industry in Canada, 2005.* www.fishharvesterspecheurs.ca/product/setting-new-course.

———. *Fisheries Seasonality and the Allocation of Labour and Skills, Labour market Information Study*, 2018. www.fishharvesterspecheurs.ca/resource-centre/library.

Community-University Research for Recovery Alliance (CURRA) at Memorial University. *Moving Forward: Building Economically, Socially and Ecologically Resilient Fisheries and Coastal Communities* (policy paper), 2014. www.curra.ca/documents/CURRA-Booklet-FINAL-WebRes.pdf.

Economic Analysis Economic Analysis and Statistics Branch, Fisheries and Oceans Canada. *Socio-economic Profile of Canada's Fishing Industry Labour Force 1994–2006.* Statistical and Economic Analysis Series. https://waves-vagues.dfo-mpo.gc.ca/Library/365755.pdf.

GSGislason & Associates. *The BC Fishing Industry—Labour Market Information, 2013.* Available from British Columbia Seafood Alliance.

GTA Consultants, for Canadian Council of Professional Fish Harvesters. *Assessing the Skills Needs of Aboriginal Fish Harvesters in Canada.* 2012. www.fishharvesterspecheurs.ca/product/assessing-skills-needs-aboriginal-fish-harvesters-canada.

3. DEMOGRAPHIC AND RURAL POPULATION CHALLENGES

Bollman, Ray D. *Rural Canada 2013: An Update, A Statement of the Current Structure and Trends in Rural Canada.* Prepared for the Federation of Canadian Municipalities. http://crrf.ca/rural-canada-2013-an-update/.

———. *Rural Demography Update 2016* (Rural Ontario Institute). www.ruralontarioinstitute.ca/file.aspx?id=26acac18-6d6e-4fc5-8be6-c16d326305fe.

Canadian Rural Revitalization Foundation. *State of Rural Canada 2015.* http://sorc.crrf.ca/.

4 BRITISH COLUMBIA FISHERIES

BC Stats. *British Columbia's Fisheries and Aquaculture Sector.* Prepared for BC Ministry of Agriculture. November 2018. https://www2.gov.bc.ca/assets/gov/farming-natural-resources-and-industry/agriculture-and-seafood/statistics/industry-and-sector-profiles/sector-reports/british_columbias_fisheries_and_aquaculture_sector_2016_edition.pdf.

Brown, Dennis. *Salmon Wars: the Battle for the West Coast Salmon Fishery* (Madeira Park, BC: Harbour Publishing, 2005).

Ecotrust Canada and the T. Buck Suzuki Environmental Foundation. *Caught Up In Catch Shares.* 2014. http://ecotrust.ca/report/caught-up-in-catch-shares/.

———. *Just Transitions: Towards Truly Sustainable Fisheries in British Columbia.* 2018 http://ecotrust.ca/wp-content/uploads/2018/11/JustTranscations_JustTransitions_Dec21.pdf.

House of Commons Standing Committee on Fisheries and Oceans. *West Coast Fisheries: Sharing Risks and Benefits.* May 2019. www.ourcommons.ca/DocumentViewer/en/42-1/FOPO/report-21/.

5 USEFUL WEBSITES

Canadian Council of Professional Fish Harvesters. fishharvesterspecheurs.ca/.

Canadian Independent Fish Harvester's Federation. fed-fede.ca/.

Coldwater Lobster Association, Yarmouth Nova Scotia. coldwaterlobster.ca/.

Ecotrust Canada. ecotrust.ca/.

Fédération Régionale Acadienne des Pêcheurs Professionnels. frapp.org/.

Fisheries and Oceans Canada (DFO). *Fisheries Policies and Frameworks.* dfo-mpo.gc.ca/reports-rapports/regs/policies-politiques-eng.htm.

Fisheries and Oceans Canada Statistics Services. Commercial Fisheries. dfo-mpo.gc.ca/stats/commercial-eng.htm.

Grand Manan Fishermen's Association. gmfa.nb.ca/.

Government of Canada. Trade Data Online. ic.gc.ca/eic/site/tdo-dcd.nsf/eng/home.

Maritimes Fishermen's Union. mfu-upm.com/.

Mi'kmaq Confederacy of Prince Edward Island (MCPEI). mikmaq.m5i.com/.

Native Brotherhood of British Columbia. nativebrotherhood.ca/.

Newfoundland and Labrador Fish Food and Allied Workers – UNIFOR: ffaw.nf.ca/.

Newfoundland and Labrador Professional Fish Harvester Certification Board. pfhcb.com/.

Oceana Canada (international environmental NGO specializing in ocean conservation). oceana.ca/en/our-mission.

Oceans North (environmental NGO specializing in fisheries and the marine ecosystem management). oceansnorth.org/en/.

Parliament of Canada. House of Commons Standing Committee on Fisheries and Oceans proceedings reports. ourcommons.ca/Committees/en/FOPO.

Parliament of Canada. Senate of Canada, Standing Committee on Fisheries and Oceans proceedings reports. sencanada.ca/en/committees/pofo/.

Prince Edward Island Fishermen's Association. peifa.org/members/home.

T. Buck Suzuki Foundation. bucksuzuki.org.

United Fishermen and Allied Workers' Union–UNIFOR, British Columbia. ufawu-unifor.org/home.html.

INDEX

Prince Edward Island 40, 42, 45, 62, 63, 75, 169

Prince Edward Island Fishermen's Association xv, 174

Prince Rupert 93

Professional Fish Harvesters Certification Board 166, 167

Q

Quebec 11, 40, 42, 49, 58, 59, 60, 62, 64, 65, 84, 85, 90, 100, 101, 108, 131, 148, 157, 166

S

Saulnier, Hubert 67

Savoie, Donald viii, xii

Scotian Shelf 149

Seafood Value Chain Roundtable 150

Service Canada 97

Shea, Gail xiii, 15, 55

Shetland Islands 149

Siddon, Tom 15

Standing Committee on Fisheries and Oceans (SCOFO) 140

Statistics Canada tax filer data 24, 25, 27, 39, 40, 41, 44, 45, 46, 57, 74, 80, 81, 83, 84, 91, 92, 103, 106, 108, 124, 126, 127, 129, 130, 135, 187

Supreme Court 128

Sweden 116

Switzerland 116

T

T. Buck Suzuki Foundation 137

Thibault, Robert 67

Tobin, Brian xiii

Transport Canada 181

U

Unemployment Insurance (UI) 71, 73, 108, 113

United Fishermen and Allied Workers' Union xv

United Kingdom 116

United Nations Human Rights Committee 163

United States 5, 149

University of Alaska 162

Unleashing the Growth Potential of Key Sectors 4

V

Vancouver Island 93

variable entrance requirements (VER) 111

W

West Coast Fisheries: Sharing Risks and Benefits 141

Western Nova Scotia Lobster Dealers Coalition 67

Wholly Owned Corporation 172, 173

Wilkinson, Jonathan 16

Woolley, Dr. Frances 121

Y

Young Fishermen's Development Act 164